PSYCHIC ATTACK

By

Draja Mickaharic

Lulu, Inc.
Raleigh, NC 27607
USA

First Published in 2012
This revision 2013 by
3101 Hillsborough St.
Raleigh, NC   27607

www.Lulu.com

© 1980 – 2012 – 2013 by
Draja Mickaharic and John M. Hansen

All rights reserved
   No part of this book may be reproduced, stored in a retrieval system, or transmitted by any means, electronic, mechanical, photocopying, recording, or otherwise, by any means known or yet to be discovered, without written permission from the author.

ISBN 978-1-300-71902 - 1
LCCN

Printed in the United States of America

PSYCHIC ATTACK

PREFACE

Psychic attack is the attempt by one person to control the thoughts, actions, decisions, or behavior of another person through punishing them psychic, or nonphysical, means. Psychic attack is always an immoral action, an act of moral malpractice, as it is an attempt by one person to control the life of another human being. Whether or not any particular psychic attack is successful, launching the attack is in itself an immoral act.

A great deal of human suffering is the direct result of psychic attack. This is especially true of those attacks that originate from those who feel that they have the right and duty to regulate the affairs of their friends, neighbors, relatives, and associates. As one of the principal lessons of life on this Earth is obtaining control of one's conscious thoughts, it is unlikely that the practice of psychic attacks will cease until humanity as a whole gains control of their conscious thoughts. Until this ideal state of affairs comes about, people need to know about, and be aware of, the damage done by even random thoughts of a malicious nature.

The control of one's mind is more honored in theory than in practice. It is a difficult art, one that must be mastered afresh in each lifetime. Because it is not something that is automatic in the development of the child, nor encouraged by the animal instinctual nature, it is likely we will have the results of mankind's mutual psychic attacks with us for quite some time. By understanding the true nature of psychic attack, we will be able to avoid at least some of the many pitfalls it holds for the unwary. We can at least identify what it is we are doing when it occurs to us we ourselves are in the process of launching a conscious attack. In addition, we may be able to identify some of the symptoms of psychic attack should we fall victim to this form of moral malpractice.

The only real remedy for deliverance from deliberate psychic attack is a personal consultation with a reputable spiritual practitioner. Should this be out of the question for some reason it is reassuring to realize that time alone will cure most of the minor and random psychic attacks one may occasionally receive.

My book Spiritual Cleansing gives a description of the first aid types of remedies for these minor attacks. Stronger attacks, the results of the unwelcome attention of a partially trained mind of malefic intent, require the work of one who is qualified to deal with them.

Anyone may remove the infrequent splinter from their hand, but it requires a certain kind of person with special knowledge and training to remove an appendix. In deciding to undertake any action of major spiritual cleansing, it is worthwhile to look into locating a qualified spiritual practitioner who can perform the work. Should you not be able to locate one, you are better off with the first aid treatment, as mentioned in this and my Spiritual Cleansing book, than dealing with someone in whom you can have no faith. Rarely does a desire to be helpful result in anything other than a great deal of foolishness, although often performed in the name of spirituality.

There is apparently some question as to just what a spiritual practitioner is. I have referred to those who perform spiritual cleansings, hoodoo spiritual work, healing, and other work of various kinds for others in this manner. One might also say that these people are the professionals of the realm of the sacred. In the English language there is no specific term for those who work in this area except the church connected word, priests and often despised title of witch. In most other, cultures, especially more primitive cultures, there exist people who work in the nonphysical realms. They are often referred to by titles that approximate the English phrase witch doctor. In their cultures, these specialists are often treated with the same awe and respect that modern Americans grant to their physicians.

There are a few cultural terms describing the kind of person to whom I referred to as a spiritual practitioner. These terms may be more familiar to those whose origins are from more directly ethnic areas. In the Pennsylvania Dutch country, these people are called Hexenmeisters. In the Puerto Rican or Cuban community, they are called Santeros. The Haitians refer to them as Hougans, while Mexicans may refer to them as Curadors. In the American black community, they are known as hoodoo workers. In England they are called cunning men, and in Italy Strega. Those who can actually supply spiritual services for their clients are not limited to the traditional or the ethnic practices but these professionals of the sacred are found among the ranks of the occultist and the mystic more than among the membership or clergy of any organized religion.

Should one prefer to consult a member of their religious practice concerning a spiritual affliction, it would be advised to seek out one who is known as a mystic. There are members of all religions who have some understanding of the spiritual and its affliction. However, they are rare, and difficult to locate. Among the Protestant Christian churches there is no one whom I have heard of who was able to deal with spiritual difficulties. Many of these men are able to pray for relief in someone, but it has been my experience that their abilities are very limited.

Members of the Church of Jesus Christ of Latter Day Saints – The Mormons - have within their church people who are familiar with the nonphysical, and who can pray successfully for the release of psychic difficulties. At one time I was acquainted with two Roman Catholic priests who were qualified spiritual practitioners unfortunately one of them has died and the other one has retired.

Those who become spiritual practitioners must literally be born for their work. In addition, they must undergo long and often arduous training to prepare themselves. These studies relate to a different realm of experience than that of the intellect, and this absolutely requires a teacher to guide the student along his path. In many cases, the student must be initiated into a specific spiritual practice. If they are intended to teach or work in this practice, this is always the case. Just as with every other field of endeavor, not all of those who claim to have the ability to do this work are actually able to do it. One sure and certain sign of a real spiritual practitioner is their lack of advertising. Those who are legitimate spiritual practitioners never advertise their services. One finds them only through word-of-mouth referrals.

Storefront readers and advisors make the greatest part of their income pretending to be spiritual practitioners. They claim to be able to remove curses and to be able to see the various influences one has on them. Few of them have the ability to either see curses or to remove them. Any person who asks a huge fee for doing something so morally necessary as are removing curses is usually not able to do the work they are promising to do. Spiritual practitioners usually charge only enough to support themselves. It is not a field in which one becomes wealthy. No matter how difficult you think your case is, you should avoid the reader and advisers who advertise themselves in every large city.

As I mentioned in my book Spiritual Cleansing, if you have earned the right to the assistance, it will be made available to you. If you have not earned the right to assistance with a spiritual problem, you must look into yourself and find out what it is within you that keeps you from being helped. Should you find that you have character defects that keep you from finding aid; you should act decisively to strengthen and improve your character. Once you have made the necessary changes within yourself, you will receive any additional assistance you may require.

Once an individual ceases to have anger and hatred directed toward others, they have begun their long and slow ascent that will ultimately bring them to a higher level of spirituality. Once they are able to realize that love and concern for their fellow man is a moral duty of all mankind, they have placed themselves out of range of any tendency to attack others psychically. At this point, they can no longer become the victim of an attack by others.

Draja Mickaharic

Feast of St. Christopher
1980 A.D.

NOTE

This book was originally written for one of Draja Mickaharic's advanced students, but is being published, with his permission, as an item of general interest.

John M. Hansen
November 2012

CONTENTS

I	Common Psychic Attack	1
II	Examples Of Common Psychic Attack	14
III	Defense Against Common Psychic Attack	30
IV	Deliberate Psychic Attack	42
V	Examples Of Deliberate Psychic Attack	55
VI	Miscellaneous Kinds Of Psychic Attack	69
VII	Psychically Attacking Yourself	79
VIII	Beginning To Train Your Mind	88
IX	Some Exercises To Train Your Mind	97
-	Some Remedies For Common Psychic Attack	102

x

1

COMMON PSYCHIC ATTACK

The most common form of psychic attack is that of the untrained mind of one person acting upon the untrained mind of another through negative thoughts, criticisms, condemnation, and complaint. Nagging and scolding are not often recognized as a form of psychic attack but they are. Whether or not these negative thoughts are verbalized is unimportant. Thoughts themselves have power, and like drops of water wearing away a stone, they will in time show the effect of their evil intention. When thoughts are verbalized, there is at least some chance the recipient will eventually say, enough! The victim may then save himself by breaking off any form of contact or communication with the person who is the source of verbal abuse. When the thoughts are not verbalized, which is more often the case, the recipient is often unaware of the other person's malefic interest in them.

Common psychic attacks usually result from emotion driven thoughts of envy, jealousy, hatred, greed, anger, or lust being transmitted from the subconscious mind of the sender to the subconscious mind of the recipient. As most people have undisciplined minds, this form of attack is far more common than we are usually willing to suppose.

PSYCHIC ATTACK

How common this negativity is in daily life can be tested by any person who wishes to keep an accurate record of how often they have any negative thoughts concerning their fellow men. Keep a record of the number of times thoughts of envy, anger, hate, jealousy, greed, or lust enters your mind during an ordinary day. This will give you some insight into how frequently negativity occurs in your own life. The result of such an experiment, honestly and objectively completed, will usually be quite a shock, and a real illumination, to the person who undertakes it. Once a person begins attempting to control their mind, they become aware of the difficulties involved in eliminating these negative thoughts. This will give them some idea of the prevalence of psychic attacks through thoughts of negativity in this world.

The idea that thoughts are things is an old chestnut to those who have studied metaphysics, the occult sciences, or Theosophy. Many people repeat this phrase lightly, without understanding the truth of it. One who has experienced the truth of the statement, that thoughts are things, will never doubt it. Thoughts an individual thinks have a life and energy of their own. Taken in their totality they shape the life of the individual, just as the thoughts of humanity as a whole shape what humanity is, at any given moment. These thoughts also provide the basis for what humanity will become in the immediate future.

Most people have no control over their thoughts. People exist alone within their consciousness, in a state of continuous mental chatter and internal conversation. This conversation has no clarity, no direction, and no real purpose. In all too many cases, the primary theme of their internal chatter is worry, self-concern, self-pity, and always negativity. In other cases, it is a stream of justifications and rationalizations, which convince the individual they are right, and the rest of the world is wrong. This is actually a form of self-generated psychic attack, which gradually takes its toll on the individual as they pass through their life.

Human minds respond almost randomly to the thoughts and mental forms surrounding them at any time. Human minds also respond to the thought patterns impressed on them by the

COMMON PSYCHIC ATTACK

forces of the nonphysical universe. Human minds respond and react to these impressions according to the habitual response patterns, existing within their memories. These patterns indicate the accepted pattern of responding to any particular stimulation presented to them. In most cases, and with most people, this stimulation and response reaction operates in much the same manner as Pavlov's dogs, salivating at the sound of a bell.

The actual procedure within the human mind is only slightly more complicated than that which is found in Pavlov's dogs. In the human mind, the actual response to any given stimulus is conditioned, not only by the stimulus that provokes the response, but also by the sum of the memories within the subconscious mind, as influenced by the particular confluence of other non-physical forces (Astral forces) acting on that human mind at the time the particular stimulus is applied.

The entire science of human mentation, including the operation of the human mind, the science of psychology, as it is known to Western civilization, was fully understood many hundreds of years ago. That this is not a part of our current cultural understanding is due more to the changes in the way we currently believe the human mind should work than it is to changes in the way the human mind actually works. Those who sincerely believe they wish to ultimately learn to work with the human mental condition should first obtain a deep understanding of the true manner of the operation of the human mind through the study and development of their own minds. This is cannot be accomplished through any academic form of mental training or therapy.

The brief and partial description of the mental action of the human mind that is given in these pages is adequate for this work, but it is not adequate for those who wish to use this information as a mental therapist or spiritual practitioner. It is as important to point out the deficiencies of this explanation, as it is to provide the explanation itself. The explanation is not be taken as complete, as this could cause the person who believes this is all there is, to do damage to themselves or those they are attempting to help. It is often said that a little knowledge is

PSYCHIC ATTACK

a dangerous thing. In the area of the mind, a little knowledge can be very damaging to the individual, as well as to those who may entrust themselves to his care.

Because most people pass through life with no directed thinking process, they exist in this fog of random thought and feeling. Any thought directed to them by another person must first past from the fog of the originators thoughts and emotions, through the fog of the thoughts and emotions of the intended recipient. As this is essentially the passage of an ill formed thought from one fog to another, there is very little clarity left in the thought when it reaches the mind of the intended recipient. Should the thought be intended to affect the conscious mind of the recipient, it then must pass the test of approval of the recipient's conscious mind. Most people will not entertain the thought of another that is definitely negative to them, as judged within their conscious mind. Negative thoughts from others turn from the conscious mind and lodge in the recipient subconscious mind. There, these thoughts are added to whatever store of negativity already exists on the same, or any similar subject.

An accumulation of a sufficient number of these negative thoughts will gradually increase the individuals's conscious negative perception of themselves. This can, and eventually will, reinforce the negative internal conversation in the person's mind. It can ultimately lead to the accumulation of enough negativity to result in the individual's becoming psychically or physically debilitated. This is the result of long exposure to the negative thoughts of others. Self-generated negative thoughts can have the same result, and can in time accumulate enough negative energy to result in the same kind of physical or psychic debilitation as constantly receiving negative thoughts from others.

The force which powers negative thoughts, and which in fact powers all thoughts, is the emotional energy generated by the person transmitting the thought. This energy is always dependent upon the emotional energy potential of the individual. The more intense the emotional energy an individual places into any thought, the more intense the energy transmitted by the thought. In the case of the spoken word

COMMON PSYCHIC ATTACK

resulting from the thought, the connection between the emotions felt and the force of speech is frequently obvious. It is not as obvious in the case of a thought that is not verbalized. Some thoughts, which have greater emotional importance for the individual, will be launched with maximum emotional energy, while other thoughts that are not as emotionally stirring to the person, will have much less energy.

In his book Psychic Energy, Joseph J. Weed observed, "In countries where emotions run high, people age quickly. Women at 35 are often old women. Men in these areas last longer, chiefly because the need to earn a living requires of them a certain amount of emotional control. On the other hand in countries where the climate is more rigorous and self-discipline is essential to survival, people grow old gracefully and more slowly."

(Page 38 - Paperback Library Edition Copyright by Parker Publishing Company, 1970. ISBN 78 – 92527)

The more emotional energy one is accustomed to using, the more emotional energy one will put into every effort, whether they be for negative or positive endeavors; whether directed to oneself, or directed to others. The corollary to this is that the more emotional energy one regularly sends out to others, the more one is willing to receive from others, whether for good or ill.

This is very much like learning to live in a certain environment. If you are used to living with a constant flux of emotional energy you will become habituated to living with it. Your response will be to use as much emotional energy as possible, whatever the situation, always using far more emotional energy than the person who is not used to living in that same emotional flux. The most self-discipline and self-contained person is used to living without the flux of emotional energy surrounding him. He would find it difficult to raise as much emotional energy to accomplish sending a thought, as a more emotional person would consider using in a casual greeting to a friend.

Those people who are completely positive in their emotional and mental attitude toward life age much more slowly than

PSYCHIC ATTACK

those who are surrounded by negativity, and accept that negativity into them. A positive mental and emotional approach to life, through a positive attitude, is clearly its own reward. A negative approach to life always increases the pain, suffering, and traumatic experiences of life, and seriously decreases their chance for future happiness. This is not being said as an advocate of Pollyanna approach to life, but to point out there is no new adversity on this earth. One can bear anything that one has to bear without becoming embittered, resentful, or negative. It is the desire of the individual to play God, to control everything and everyone around them, which makes life so difficult. By understanding that submission to the will of God is simply allowing what will be to be, the desire to control others can be dispensed with.

Negative thoughts from others that have a direct bearing upon the emotional causes important to the one sending them have the greatest amount of emotional energy in them. They are usually thoughts that involve obsessions, fixations, strong habitual thought patterns, and strong emotional commitments. Jealousy and envy of another person's good fortune are examples of these thoughts. Jealousy and envy both play upon the belief that what another person has should belong to the jealous one. These are always distracting emotions, although not often even recognize consciously. In some cases, the emotion of envy and greed can manifest as a particularly strong and overwhelming feeling. When a person has a fixation or obsession about jewelry, for example, to see another person wearing, a piece of jewelry which the jealous person covets can cause a feeling which is very close to physical pain.

The spiritual affliction known as Malochia, or the evil eye, is an example of an affliction caused by jealousy and envy on the part of one person for another's good fortune or possessions. This affliction has its origin in the subconscious mind of the sender and is usually powered by a fixation or obsession that the individual deserves far more material wealth than they have received. It translates as a punishment toward the receiving person for having something the sender of the affliction feels they deserve. As this affliction is usually transmitted, it passes from the subconscious mind of the sending person to the

COMMON PSYCHIC ATTACK

subconscious mind of the receiving person without passing through the conscious mind of either. Although originating in the Mediterranean basin, this affliction is so common in all societies it has a chapter of its own in my book Spiritual Cleansing.

As the subconscious mind of the average untrained person is not under the control of his or her conscious mind, the subconscious mind will accept without question any thought or energy sent to it from anyone. It will also accept uncritically negative energies that are sent to it from the conscious mind in the form of discouragements, criticisms, and general ill feeling. These thoughts are compared to the memory stored in the subconscious mind. If there are present any similar negative thoughts, or any negative programs in the form of emotional belief structures, these negative thoughts are acted on by the person, in accordance with the memories stored within their subconscious mind.

Despite all the works of popular psychology on the subject, few people are able to make contact with their subconscious mind as being separate from their conscious mind. Fewer people yet are able to learn to control their subconscious mind. Until the subconscious mind has a program or instruction in the form of a belief pattern within it that denies entry to negative thoughts from others, it will accept whatever thought is sent to it, either by the conscious mind or by an outside source. It will receive the thought without question, and without notifying the conscious mind of its receipt in any way. Before the conscious mind can be notified of the receipt of thoughts, and given the opportunity to accept or reject them, there must be a certain harmony between the conscious and subconscious minds of the individual. Further, the subconscious mind must have a strong belief pattern within it indicating the conscious mind is the agent whose decision must prevail in the matter.

Once negative thought images come to the conscious mind, they are usually severely edited through the rational faculty before they are transmitted, either verbally or as conscious thoughts. This process of editing occurs not because of any moral enlightenment of the individual residing in their rational

PSYCHIC ATTACK

faculty, but because in order to be verbalized it is necessary that the thought be compared to the memories of the subconscious mind. Any inhibiting programs that would work against the transmission of the thought must be responded to before the thought can pass out of the subconscious mind into the conscious mind. Most people think in either words or images. This requires the words or images in which the person thinks be properly arranged before the thought can be passed into the conscious mind. In this manner, the thought is edited.

The self-discipline of the average individual and their desire to harmonize themselves with their social cultural patterns block out the transmission of most of their inherent negative energies, no matter how strong their emotional feelings are on any subject. This operates not only with the transmission of Malochia, which is found most frequently in those cultures that allow free emotional reign, but also in such fields as the acceptance of a scientific theory by those who have a decided emotional investment in the retention of formally held theories. In the latter instance, the presentation of an acceptable concept in the subconscious can block the acceptance into the belief structure of a new or unacceptable concept. The result is that this new concept can best be dealt with in the conscious mind only in terms of refutation. The objective scientist then finds they cannot cogitate upon a new and emotionally threatening theory except in terms of refutation.

When individual loses all emotional control, as in a situation of stress and anger, their words reflect their loss of control. The amount of emotional energy released through their words is never as great as the amount of emotional energy generated within them by the emotional turbulence their loss of control brings. The remaining emotional energy still clings to them after their emotional outburst has passed away. Only time will cause this residue of emotional energy to either die away or be absorbed by the person. If the person absorbs the remaining emotional energy, it will manifest within them in one of two ways. The energy can manifest either as a directed feeling of negativity to another living being, usually the one to whom they directed their words of anger when they lost their emotional control, or it can result in undirected feeling of negativity which

COMMON PSYCHIC ATTACK

will usually resound on the person themselves.

Only those who can release their negative energies will lose them entirely. These people will neither pass them on to another person, nor draw them back into themselves. To be able to release the energies of the emotions requires internal mental clarity and the ability to work with oneself through working with their subconscious mind. In other words, it requires a certain kind of training.

The formation of a negative thought in the conscious mind of an individual is the prelude to either verbalization of the thought or taking action on the thought. By the time the thought has presented itself to the individual's conscious mind, it has already been depleted of the greater amount of psychic energy through being compared to the inhibiting programming of the individual's subconscious mind. We made the state that there are three forces at work before the thought can be either verbalized or acted upon.

First - The individual feels or emotes that the prevailing circumstances allow them to verbalize or act upon the thought that is presented to them.

Second - The individual finds the thought in harmony with the programming and beliefs of their subconscious mind, and in the circumstances, a thought they can either verbalize or act upon.

Third - the individual feels or emotes that the particular circumstances can be remedied or improved through their verbalization of the thought, or through their acting upon the thought.

These same forces are at play whether we are considering a shouting match between two people arguing over the merits of the baseball team, or two attorneys arguing in court. They applied to all cases of thoughts in which the faculty of the rational mind is not involved in the selection of the thoughts, or modification of the words and phrases of the verbalized thought. In this event, the faculty of the rational mind's will is entirely dormant, and the emotional nature alone is operating

PSYCHIC ATTACK

the organism.

It is important to realize the release of a thought through verbalization or action is the launching of an effort indicative of the individual's entire moral development. That this is so has nothing whatever to do with the kind or quality of the language employed in the verbalization. In addition, this is true whether the thought ever is either verbalized or acted upon. Once the thought enters the conscious mind it is manifested. Speaking or acting upon the thought is only the final act of the drama leading to that end.

An understanding of the processes of thought is revealing, in that it indicates the requirements for a mental therapist. Unless a therapist is able to completely deal with the conscious thoughts of an individual who comes to them as a client, they will have real difficulty in treating mental illness. For a spiritual practitioner the first requirement is that they are able to read another individuals thought processes, without harming them or disrupting the train of thought of their conscious mind. Once an individual can successfully demonstrate this ability, they may be able to be trained to perform mental therapy.

This whole process begins with having complete control of one's own thoughts, which understandably requires a great deal of knowledge about one's thinking process, and thus a fully developed knowledge of oneself. It also requires having obtained a harmonization, or at least a close cooperation, between their conscious and subconscious minds. This is something that may not be taught academically. It is also a state that not every person may achieve, regardless of their desire to achieve it.

Because of the lack of control of the thought process itself, and because most people desire far more from life in the way of goods, services, and affection than they ever attain, the majority of people project negative thoughts outward from themselves, and inward into themselves, in an almost constant stream. The metal fog within which they ordinarily involve themselves acts in disbursing these thoughts as a physical fog disperses a beam of light. That the negativity with which most people surround themselves act as a barrier to their achieving

COMMON PSYCHIC ATTACK

any of the goals with which they have set for themselves should be obvious. This is one of the reasons why many self help courses, teaching people to think positively, have such resounding success. Once a person begins to speak and act in a positive instead of a negative way, they begin to aim their conscious thoughts in that direction. This process alone is enough to begin to give the individual some degree of mental clarity. At the very least, it begins to assist them in the dispersal of their surrounding fog of negativity.

One of the earliest of these positive thinking courses is still one of the best. This is the <u>Dale Carnegie Course In Public Speaking</u>. While not as popular among the masses as once it was, it is a course which has done more to dissipate negative thinking, and to clear away the fog of negativity from those who complete it, than 10,000 sermons by the religious. Using practical techniques in learning how to understand people it has become almost a requirement for anyone who wishes to make a success of their life. Those who feel they have any difficulty interrelating with their fellow human beings should certainly consider taking this excellent course.

The amount of negativity that is found in those who have the greatest mental power is less than that found in society as a whole. Those who pass through life with a positive and enthusiastic outlook on life are those who overcome adversity not only with joy, but with real happiness. Being happy in the face of adversity is the best way to defeat adversity. Actually, once you can recognize you are in conscious control of your emotional state at any time, you may use that knowledge to maintain a happy approach to life no matter what life brings.

From the above considerations, we may rightly conclude that mental negativity forms a sort of constant background against which the drama of life is played out. We may have become so accustomed to the presence of negativity in our lives we barely notice it. We simply accept it as a part of our daily life, and thus invite it into us. Gradually, as the individual grows to maturity, it may begin to occur to them is no longer necessary to accept negativity from those individuals who with whom they find themselves in daily contact. This begins,

PSYCHIC ATTACK

usually, as a defense concept in the conscious mind, and is often the result of connecting a particularly damaging negative concept accepted by the subconscious mind to a particular sender. It might be summarized as the following example shows.

> George and Ethel are a married couple. George continually nags Ethyl about her housework, appearance, etc., etc.
> Ethel, because of a particularly heavy and emotionally traumatic criticism session decides she no longer has to accept George's complaints and nagging.

NOTE: This is a conscious decision of her rational mind. Its acceptance by her subconscious mind is based upon her prior programming, which will determine how her subconscious mind will deal with the situation.

The variety of responses Ethel will have to this decision of her conscious mind will depend upon a large number of factors, and is not completely predictable. If she has actually made the conscious decision to change her prior behavior in regard to George, she will begin immediately following this decision to exhibit changed behavior. That this may also include directing acts of violence toward George is beyond question. The first step however is her refusal to accept any further negativity from George.

Once an individual learns on a deep subconscious level they no longer have to accept any negative energy from anyone, they are no longer subject to them. In fact, this usually takes a lifetime to accomplish, and is not often found to happen instantaneously. While this development is the goal of many people, it is an essential truth, for no one has the right to interfere in the life of another human being, to send them negative influences, thoughts of control, or thoughts restricting them in any way.

One of the constants in almost all societies is that those who are members of the society feel they have the right to transmit not only negative thoughts to others, but to use negative words

COMMON PSYCHIC ATTACK

and actions to correct what they individually perceived as antisocial behavior on the part of others. Once an individual realizes they no longer have to receive negative energy from someone else, they usually ceased to transmit, at least verbally, negative energies to others. The fog of negativity in which most people live their lives has no silver lining. Indeed, it is the principal cause of human suffering on this Earth. This is the reason the poet has stated, "Most people live lives of quiet desperation."

We have reviewed the mechanism by which negative thoughts manifest in the common psychic attack. The difference between the powerful but wholy subconscious process of Malochia and the less powerful but conscious process of negative mentation, verbalization, and action has been covered. We will now examine some typical cases of common psychic attack and see how this malefic process operates in daily life.

PSYCHIC ATTACK

2

SOME EXAMPLES OF COMMON PSYCHIC ATTACK

Because common psychic attack is essentially surrounding an individual with negative thoughts, the closer proximity the victims maintains to the aggressor, the stronger the force of the attack manifests. Any individual who maintains close proximity to a person who is habituated to negative thinking is very likely to become a victim of common psychic attack.

One of the most frequent situations for continuous psychic attack is the human pair bond. When any couple lives together over a long period of time, there is an accumulation of unresolved negative experiences between them. This accumulated negativity is one of the primary causes of tension in any pair bond relationship. Should one of the partners in the pair bond hold a grudge against the other partner, they will direct negativity at their partner because of the unresolved frictions and tensions in the relationship.

The desire to marry to have a permanent mate is socially programmed into both men and women. The biological programming for sexual release provides one of the strongest power drives in the human being. It is so strong it can be frustrated in normal human beings only through exceptional circumstances. Cultural programming in all societies directs a strong natural biological sexual drive toward the culturally approved condition of marriage, which implies a production of children. This program is made a part of every child as it matures. It is an anticipation program, which directs a child to eventually take their place in society as adults.

This program in every society is directed to conforming the child to the unexpressed but real desires of the society, or the state, for a constant population base, which has respect for the authority of the parent, and, by transference as adults, for the authority of the state. Implicit in the anticipation programming of the married state is the implication that once a person is married, or has a family, and is thus an adult, they will be able to fulfill all of their expectations.

These expectations usually include, but are not limited to, financial security, happy loving children, approval of both sets of parents, approval of society as a whole, and the final and complete acceptance by all of the authority figures one admires as having attended full adult status. In addition, implied within the anticipation programming is a belief that only within the bonds of the married pair bond can they have their sexual desires fully realized.

Understanding the expectations and anticipations of the married state are rarely realized, can be seen by picking any marriage one knows of at random and objectively examining it. Honest discussions with the members of the marital pair bond, separately and privately, invariably reveal either an unfeeling façade hardened by lost expectations and role-playing, or the loss of illusions about the married state. The older the partners were at the time of marriage, the more likely they are to accept the many adjustment problems presented by marriage. However, even the acceptance of the difficulties inherent in marriage is not a guarantee of freedom from the presence of psychic attack. So far as I am aware there is never been a marriage that was fully satisfying to both members of the marital pair bond over the length of its life.

SOME EXAMPLES OF COMMON PSYCHIC ATTACK

That such a situation is ripe for the internal and unvoiced struggle of mutual common psychic attack is obvious. Mutual psychic attack is always detrimental to the pair bond, materially as well as emotionally. The material loss occasioned by mutual exchanges of negativity brings another source of friction to the pair bond, which only increases the incidence of psychic attack. The personal and sexual relationship between the two partners can only grow worse as mutual psychic attack continues.

With negativity piled on negativity and attack following attack, the ultimate result is the destruction of the marriage. At the very least, it will result in the complete destruction of the relative importance of one partner in the marriage. The nature of the result depends upon the relative power and malevolence of the people concerned. In the end, the most directly malefic person will manage to break the least malevolent person in the marriage. As an example of what can happen in a pair bond situation, the following example should suffice. The example is given in detail as I have watched it develop over the last 15 years. The names have been changed but the story is not only true it is actually quite typical.

Ethel married George shortly after they graduated from high school. Both families, who were well acquainted from living in the same neighborhood and attending the same church, endorsed their marriage. George had found Ethel the most obliging of the few women with whom he had any kind of sexual contact. He desired to have regular and frequent sexual contact with her, and this was the basis for his desire to marry her. Ethel had a strong desire to get married to escape her mother's home, and domination. Once Ethel and George were married, they settled down within walking distance of both their parents' homes.

Fathers who worked at low-level clerical positions supported both parents' families. George obtained a similar position working with motor freight invoices. He quickly settled into the role he assumed was the husband's role, learned from observing his father and his few married friends. Ethel settled into the busy housewife role, cooking, cleaning, and decorating, she had learned from her mother.

PSYCHIC ATTACK

Ethel had always considered herself a beautiful gracious and sophisticated young woman. She had assumed that marriage would bring to her all the material rewards she desired, even surpassing those her mother had accumulated over the many years of her marriage. It seemed to her the life she desired was to be hers at first, as she and George spent a two-week honeymoon at a resort matching her anticipation of the manner she wished to spend her life. Once she was settled into the routine of housework, with frequent days spent with either her mother or her mother-in-law, she soon learned her anticipations about life after marriage were at fault. These anticipations were slowly replaced in her conscious mind by a growing resentment of her husband. She began to make mental notes of all the things George did she disapproved of.

George, for his part, found every day much like every other day. His weekends he spent working on their apartment or working with his father or father in law on theirs. Sunday's they attended church, which was always followed by dinner with either his or Ethel's parents. George had always fancied himself a dashing adventurers man whose talents would soon be recognized, bringing him to the top of any business in which he cared to apply himself. He began to feel he was spending himself on unrewarding and monotonous tasks; simply so Ethel could lounge around the house. He resented having to work at a boring job to earn his family a living.

They had not been married very long when Ethel became pregnant. After accepting the social acclaim her condition brought her, she began to have grave doubts about the idea of having a baby. She had become an accepted into the circle of married women in her neighborhood, but their stories of motherhood were not reassuring to her, and Ethel began to have direct negative thoughts about George for making her pregnant. These thoughts fueled her growing resentment of him. Ethel began to criticize George openly when they were alone. In public, she began using negative phrases toward him whenever the opportunity offered.

George was unsure about becoming a father. While outwardly proud he was to become a father, he was not looking forward to the increased drain on his income a child would

SOME EXAMPLES OF COMMON PSYCHIC ATTACK

bring. As the pregnancy advanced, his not being able to have sexual contact with Ethel bothered him as well. He began to resent the unborn child, and he began to resent Ethel for conceiving it.

During a discussion of finances shortly before the baby was born, Ethel criticized George for not making enough money at his job. George became consciously aware she had become critical of him, adding fuel to his resentment of Ethel. The following day, while talking with another man at work, George suddenly realized his anticipations of what life would be like after marriage was not going to be realized. He mentally compared his condition to that of a few of his peers who were single, and understood that to him, they had a better life. Instead of realizing that his anticipations were socially programmed, he decided the only reason his anticipations were not being fulfilled was that Ethel was blocking him from them. He mentally placed all of the responsibility for his disappointment squarely on Ethel's shoulders.

After the baby was born, George began to openly criticize Ethel in private. When she criticized him, he used arguments in rebuttal against her. He criticized her about the child; it's noise, and her lack of care for it. Ethel on the other hand found herself tired and worn from caring for the child, and began to criticize George more openly. George's income was Ethel's main complaint, particularly as the financial strain of the addition of the baby to their family began to tell.

When the baby was about six months old, George suffered a severe setback on his job. The entire procedure of the job was to be changed, and George was not sure he could adapt to the new procedure. George returned home that evening, almost in a state of shock from the news he had received. Ethel recognized his depleted state, and instead of being emotionally supportive, she took advantage of it by insisting that George complete a minor repair job he had set aside for the weekend. She was unresponsive to his trying to tell her about the changes in his job, and she denied his later request for sexual gratification. Instead, she complained to him about his low income, calling his job stupid, and she criticized his masculinity.

PSYCHIC ATTACK

All of Ethel's blows hit George at a time when he was in a state of emotional shock over changes at his job. At such times, he would usually collapse into himself or attempt to armor himself against Ethel. This time, feeling the blows she delivered, George consciously decided mentally that he would no longer take any more abuse from Ethel. Consciously, George was considering a divorce, which would have alienated him from his family and friends. Subconsciously, he was erecting a barrier to Ethel's negativity.

The following weekend, George spoke openly and frankly with his father. This conversation revealed to him that his expectations and anticipations of married life were entirely false. He became very disillusioned about his father's place in the world because of this conversation. His father pointed out that divorce was not the answer, and that he was, and had been, in the same position as George. His father, whom George had always admired and respected, had showed another side of himself to his son. George felt his father had lied to him about what you could expect in life, as well as in marriage. After George returned home and thought out the discussion with his father, he began to resent his father's influence in his life. George began to blame his father for his marriage as well as his beliefs and behavior patterns.

Being unwilling to accept any responsibility for the condition he found himself in, George transferred all the blame for his condition to Ethel and his parents. Because he really felt himself innocent of any responsibility, he enforced his self-conscious decision to refuse to accept any of Ethel's negativity. Soon he was able to expand this and extend this decision to his and her parents. The decision to refuse to accept negativity from anyone was in effect extended from just Ethel to the entire universe. While this closed George off completely to Ethel, it conflicted with the programs he had internalized about his parents being major authority figures in his life. These programs were too strong to be easily cast aside.

Consciously, George began to brood about his wife, focusing an almost continual stream of negativity toward her. He mentally criticized her parents, her appearance, her speech, her housekeeping, her cooking, and her sexual performance. He

SOME EXAMPLES OF COMMON PSYCHIC ATTACK

criticized the way she cared for their child, both mentally and openly. He became aware of her picking at him in public, and started responding to her in kind. He intensified his rebuttal of her private criticism of him, and added detailed criticism of his own. What had actually happened in their marriage was that the two partners had opened a psychic war on each other, in which the only weapon was mental psychic attack, thinly disguised by verbal sparring matches.

It would be easy to say these two people had never learned to communicate with each other. However, they both believed their mutual complaint sessions were communication. Neither of them took any responsibility for their actions. They were both more interested in finding and fixing a source to blame than they were in remedying any condition in their marriage. The couple was obviously on a downhill track. It became obvious to their parents they had to straighten things out.

At this point, through the intervention of their parents, the two combatants spoke to their parish priest. This conversation had a direct positive result, in that it was a direct application of social pressure from neutral source of higher authority in the community. Because of this intervention, there was an immediate cessation of public dissension between Ethel and George. There was also effort made in private to remedy some of the outstanding grievances of the marriage. Once these issues were settled, their private battles decreased, but only slightly.

Through the efforts of her mother, Ethel, her mother, and her mother-in-law visited the parish priest for a consultation about sex. Ethel was informed in no uncertain terms that she could not deny George use of her body. This was reinforced by a later visit with her mother, her mother-in-law, and some of the neighborhood women, who graphically and explicitly told Ethel just how she was expected to handle her husband sexual desires. As the woman leading the discussion held an important place in the church and the community, Ethel was forced into a mentally compliant attitude.

George became active in the church men's group in which his father was active. He began to take greater interest in his

PSYCHIC ATTACK

child. After a year or so his job problems smoothed out, he had adapted to the new system much easier than he had expected. George became as adept at the new monotony as he had been at the old. Ethel's cessation of sexual denial perked up his spirits a bit as well. George felt that he was on the right track in life at last.

Ethel began developing migraine headaches. While they were intermittent, they were severe. Within the next two years, she had three miscarriages, and it was necessary for her to have surgery for removal of ovarian cysts. Ethel compensated by lavishing attention on their child. Occasionally she found it necessary to take to her bed with migraine headaches, which often lasted most of the day. Ethel's headaches grew in frequency and severity, usually starting with a stinging or burning sensation in her eyes.

When their marriage reached the five-year mark, they were thought to be an ideal couple in the community. They had received community social approval, and were doing reasonably well both socially and economically. Ethel had been fully accepted as a mother by all the women in the neighborhood. Occasionally she was asked to fill responsible social roles. Her frequent headaches limited her ability to do so, but she did what she could.

George received a promotion on his job and was made a low-level supervisor. He now had three other clerks under him. He had become an important member of his church, and had joined a religious lodge as well as the men's club that his father belonged to. He was well thought of in the neighborhood, and was the recipient of considerable sympathy from those in the community who understand his wife's condition.

When their marriage had reached a seven-year mark Ethel almost constantly suffered from migraine headaches. In addition, she frequently suffered from nausea. She had developed an assortment of other illnesses, and was usually in a mental daze. She had lost her figure and had gained considerable weight. George actively resented all of these changes in her, but he did not mention his resentment publicly. In public, George treated her carefully, almost as if she were

SOME EXAMPLES OF COMMON PSYCHIC ATTACK

fragile, and certainly as if she were not able to manage her own affairs. George had put Ethel on an allowance, and he was now able to criticize her handling of the household money. George started a private savings account, and had given Ethel false information about his last two pay raises. George was determined to punish Ethel for what he felt was her ruining his life. At no time was George willing to admit he had any part in the control of his life.

George's attitude toward Ethel was exacerbated when a high school friend who had completed college, but was still single, was brought into the company as the assistant comptroller. His friend was obviously receiving a considerably higher salary than George. The fact that his high school friend was quite friendly to George only added to the inner tension between George and Ethel. George secretly thought of himself as being in his friends place, had he not married Ethel.

On another level of being, Ethel was receiving the full force of her own negativity, the energy having no outlet in George. She was also receiving the full force of George's subconscious and conscious negativity.

George made two decisions, which he was using to guide his life. Firstly, he had decided that he did not have to accept any negativity at all from Ethel, and very little from anyone else. Secondly, he had decided that everything that was wrong in his life, or could go wrong in his life, was Ethel's fault. Wrong was defined by his personal definition of wrong. He really believed Ethel had planed all of the disasters, real and imaginary, which he felt were the plagues of his life. George was actively taking out on Ethel his dislike of anything and everything that frustrated him in any way.

~§~

This delightful couple lives in close proximity to me. The prognosis of their relationship is easy to see. Ethel will grow sicker in time, and eventually as her physical body is weakened by George's metal onslaughts, she will go to an early grave. George will resent that as well. He will receive pity as a loving husband who did all they could for his poor wife. Ethel's illnesses have already given George a certain status in the

PSYCHIC ATTACK

neighborhood. Many of the neighbors consider George something of a saint for his public care of Ethel. After George goes through a period of mourning for Ethel, he will probably marry again, to give their child a mother. We shall see if he starts this new marriage with a block against accepting negativity from his new wife.

It does not matter which is of the two partners in the pair bond decide first to stop accepting negativity from the other. Whichever partner does so will usually emerge the undeclared winner in the undeclared war between them, that often is the psychic struggle of marriage. It is not that marriage must become a psychic battleground, but rather that it becomes one because of the inability of the communicants of the marriage openly try to communicate their real wants and needs to each other. This is compounded by the fact that few people today actually accept responsibility for their own actions.

Ideally, no one should marry until they have accepted full responsibility for their actions in life, and learned to enter into a free and honest communication with at least one member of the opposite sex. Role-playing should be left for the stage. People who wish to raise children in a marriage must be able to accept themselves as correctly as they can see themselves. They must also be able to accept full responsibility, in their own eyes, for their actions and for raising their children. Only at this point are people able to communicate an effective and real manner with themselves, much less with other people.

Next to common psychic attack in a pair bond or marriage, the next most frequent type of psychic attack is between a parent and a child. In these cases is more common for the parent to do psychic injury to the child than vice versa. Occasionally a child with a malefic spirit is born into a family and proceeds to attack the parent psychically. This is less common, although often more dramatic. In all my years of practice, I have seen this condition only once, and have heard about it only a few times.

A parent who has never consciously cursed their child is rare indeed. The effect of the parental curse can be strong, especially once a child is able to understand the words being

SOME EXAMPLES OF COMMON PSYCHIC ATTACK

spoken. Children are usually taught that their parents are the ultimate authority figures. Even after the child matures is difficult for the child to internally (subconsciously) deny the parents right to send it negativity. The child imprints itself upon a parent and then proceeds to pattern itself after that parent in many ways. Because of the nature of the parent as the prime authority figure, it is very difficult for the child to rid itself of the authority of the imprinting parent without doing extensive internal examination and analysis. This is to say without assistance from a therapist or another outside individual.

Once the child as a baby is brought into the home, it is liable to be the victim of passive mental psychic attack from anyone it disturbs. Newborn children, being as they are, usually attract a number of minor psychic attacks from their parents, neighbors, relatives, and siblings. Rivalry for parental attention among siblings is usually limited to subconscious negativity. Occasionally the rivalry will be verbalized, but often, even then, it is of little effect. The psychological damage it does to the child is of more importance than the psychic damage. The greatest negativity directed to a child all is usually from the oldest to the second child. By the time the third child is born there seems to be a sort of tacit acceptance by the oldest child that they can do nothing about the new babies coming into the home.

The fact that conscious curses are recognized as having less effect than subconscious malochia can be understood by looking at the variety of ways in which charms are used to protect babies and small children. These charms and prepared dolls are all used to protect the child from the effects of envy and Malochia. Little if anything is done to protect the babies from the effect of conscious curses. Malochia is usually recognized by the culturally trained practitioner as being an action of the subconscious mind. The practitioner may tell their client it is consciously directed however, for purposes of their own. Malochia can be diverted or protected against with charms, amulets, and prepared dolls. Conscious curses that have no great strength behind them may also be protected against in this way.

PSYCHIC ATTACK

As a child grows it is subject to the negativity of the minds of those around it. This negativity is rarely directed at the child unless for some real or pretended offense. In the case of an elevated soul, the child learns to turn off the negative influences in the atmosphere that surrounds it. If the child cannot refuse these influences, it usually develops bronchial or sinus difficulties. In children under seven or eight years old, this is a sign the child does not like the atmosphere in which it finds itself. After this age, frequent and prolonged colds usually show the presence of psychic negativity surrounding the child.

In some cases, one of the parents actively resents the child coming into their life. I have seen any number of cases in which both parents directed both conscious and subconscious psychic attacks to their child. Frequently the parents justify this by rationalizing that the child disturbed what the parent felt was their place in the marital relationship. This happens most often when the parents have been married in excess of three years before the first child is born. There is no one parent more likely to attack the child psychically than the other.

It is a serious mistake to believe that parents always love their children, or that children always love their parents.

When a parent actively resents a child, it usually begins as a thought that is suppressed because it is not in accordance with their subconscious programming. Once this resentment is placed into the internal memory of the subconscious however, it builds and promotes the growth of negative feelings between the parent and child, which may manifest later in life.

When a child enters into, and as it passes through, puberty, it is subject to the receipt of negative influences from both parents. The parent sees a child going into adulthood, and they see themselves aging. There are usually directed thoughts of jealousy and envy from the parent to the child at this time.

This rivalry is particularly strong in the mother-daughter relationship, as in our society a woman is valued only while she maintains her youthful appearance. The mother senses the rivalry for her husband's attention the prepubescent or pubescent woman who is her daughter presents. The usual reaction of the mother toward her daughter is one of jealousy,

SOME EXAMPLES OF COMMON PSYCHIC ATTACK

which often manifests as a continuous transmission of either psychic negativity, or malochia from the mother to the daughter.

In those few remaining cultures where the father regularly defloriates his daughter, it has happened that the wife finds herself replaced in the marital bed by her daughter at this time. Although education has practically eliminated this difficulty, the idea might still be found in the mind of the father, the mother, or both. Whether or not it is an idea or a fact, it will result in a more conscious and directed flow of negativity from the mother to daughter.

Once the child reaches a stage where it is ready to leave home, psychic negativity transmitted from the parent to the child is usually hidden under the cover a legitimate concern for the welfare of the child. In the case of the parent who stretches this concern for the child to the limit, it is often a fear the child may succeed while the parent considers they have failed. Many parents feel they have an automatic right to control the life of the child forever. The parents do not realize that their image of the child is the image they recall of the helpless newborn baby.

On any level of spiritual development, it is a truth that no human being has a right to control another human being. There is no reason or rationality that bars this from being true. The truth is constantly violated by well-meaning parents who use the excuse that they are only interested in the suppose welfare of their child. The attempts of the parents, when successful, usually lead to the parents diverting the child from their destiny in life. This earns the parents a great deal of debt toward the child, which must eventually be paid off. Control of the child, especially control after adulthood, is actually the worst form of psychic attack between the parents and their child. Unfortunately is also one of the most common.

The tie of control between parent and child can only be broken when the child realizes it must separate itself from its parent or parents for its own growth and survival. The separation that comes about in this manner is usually traumatic for both parent and child. Until the child is finally able to

PSYCHIC ATTACK

release the negative programming implanted into it in its early years, there will always be a psychic draw from the parent for it to return to parental control.

In only about two thirds of parent and child relationships does a parent see the child attain its majority. Not death but divorce and separation cause this. The desire of the parent to exert total control over the life of the child is exerted by a parent who incorrectly behaves as if they will never die. The parent also usually believes that they have the right to dictate the child's life because they have "given it birth." In fact, the only part the parents play in bringing the child into birth is the animal function. This is on the same level as a cat birthing her kittens in a field or alley. Despite all of their pretenses to the contrary, parents are not God, and they have no right to attempt to usurp the divine function, especially with regard to their children.

Another form of, psychic attack is found among those who work together. This is most noticeable among men who are in any form of low or middle level administrative or management position. As women are now often employed at this level, we should soon see this kind of psychic attack among them as well. Men in these positions attack each other almost constantly, both subconsciously and with consciously directed thoughts and words. In addition, they overly jockey for position with their bosses and subconsciously attack each other through rumor and innuendo.

Competition for certain positions in business is so great that it is not unknown for men at this level to seek the advice of someone to assist them in their plans, and work in harmony with them to assist them in their climb to the top through magical means. In some situations, this may be done with the man's wife working in harmony with him to deliberately and effectively assist him in the destruction of his competitors. In these instances, we are more often dealing with deliberate psychic attack, which we shall look into later. Never the less, the stresses in the workplace from common psychic attack can be intense.

Some examples of this include:

SOME EXAMPLES OF COMMON PSYCHIC ATTACK

A known alcoholic became so drunk at a company party he could hardly stand. He was a great embarrassment to the company officer who hired him, and with whom he displayed great familiarity in his drunken state. This caused him to lose status in the company, and turned the man who had hired him against him. His being brought into the company had caused a great deal of resentment and hate to be directed to him by a number of men who had hoped to be promoted to the position which he had been brought in to fill.

The director of a corporate research department became so mentally confused through the actions of his assistant that he was no longer able to think clearly. He made many errors of judgment on projects of a speculative nature, which eventually led to his reassignment within the company. His assistant obtained his position.

A secretary psychically attacked another woman who was an executive secretary in the same firm. This attack was personally motivated. The victim developed the typical symptoms of Malochia to the point where she frequently missed work. She was healed through treatment, and given protection against further attacks, which were then returned to their sender.

A middle level manager suffered almost continuous back pains at work. His condition became so serious that he required almost monthly medical care. This resulted in his being removed from consideration for promotion to a higher level. He was under continuous negative attack from his wife at home, and in addition, he was being psychically attacked by one of his coworkers who hated him.

The competition between salesmen in the same firm is usually intense. This is especially true when salesmen do not have clear-cut territories and sales quotas. Often management may encourage this competition under the idea that the best man will win. Unfortunately, the competition also contains large elements of Malochia and negative psychic attack directed from one salesman to the other. This can make the unaware and unprotected salesmen an immediate victim to the negativity. In these circumstances, the best man usually leaves, because he

PSYCHIC ATTACK

senses what is happening.

Competition between women on the job is as strong as it is between men. Malochia seems to play a larger part in the competition between women, not because men are more honorable by any means. Is because men will usually admit to others they want to get the SOB. Men then proceed to work consciously against someone, while women seem to have more difficulty admitting they want to get someone, unless it concerns gaining the attentions of a man.

Some people feel that of psychic attack is a rarity in life. True directed psychic attack is a rarity and directed psychic attack by a trained mind is very rare. However, as I have tried to show here, psychic attack by negative thoughts is quite common. This type of attack it is not a thrust, it brings one down but the steady drip of negativity that acts as a caustic wearing away whatever defenses the individual has until they finally succumb to its pernicious influence.

Psychic attack is usually found in any situation in which envy or jealousy is present. These include social and sporting events as well as religious meetings and anything that gives cause to excite the envy or jealousy of one human being for another. There is no place, where common psychic attack cannot occur. It is present in every form and class of society and among all cultural groups.

Until one is able to raise their spiritual nature to a point where they are beyond all thoughts of envy, jealousy, greed, anger, and hatred, is necessary to learn to defend yourself from the negativity of other people. Treatment for this common psych attack is covered in a first aid manner in the rear of this book, as well as in my book <u>Spiritual Cleansing</u>.

In the next chapter we will examine the mental approaches that may be used to free oneself of the psychic negativity that comes from within, as well as that sent to us by others.

3

DEFENSE AGAINST COMMON PSYCHIC ATTACK

Most people believe their thoughts have no origin other than within their own minds. In the two previous chapters, we have taken notice that this belief is not true. We have noted a person can actually physically succumb to the negative thoughts of others, or the negative atmosphere that surrounds them. The case of the married couple we have called George and Ethel was given at length, not because it is unique, but because it is so common. Mutual negativity, destructive to the relationship, is more often found within relationships than not.

We have seen George's determined refusal to accept any further negative from Ethel was what gave him the necessary protection he required to take the offensive psychically. While he gravely injured Ethel by doing so, the damage was due to his own lack of spirituality. It is quite possible for a person to refuse to accept negativity from others, and dissipate it, without projecting negativity onto others.

When an individual makes an irrevocable decision to deny something access to him, he will have created within himself a sufficient amount of protection to fulfill that decision. George

PSYCHIC ATTACK

made this decision because his conscious and subconscious minds were in pain from the negativity Ethel had been sending him. His decision to refuse to accept further negativity from her was accepted easily by his subconscious mind, as it made it possible for his subconscious mind to refuse further pain. His subconscious mind already had created a program about accepting negativity from his parents, so his subconscious mind did not fully accept the program that it no longer had to accept any negativity from them.

What George did was to implant belief pattern in his subconscious mind. This is one kind of defense against common psychic attack. It is known as implanting a belief pattern. For the average person without a trained mind, or the time and desire to train their mind, it is probably the best type of mental defense against common psychic attack. In many ways, it is similar to self-hypnosis, in that a strong, fixed, and essentially positive belief is firmly planted within the subconscious mind. As most peoples strong belief patterns and programs are implanted into the subconscious mind in a rather casual manner during the period between birth and four to seven years of age, the act of deliberately planting a belief pattern will usually make it one of the pillars of the persons being.

Those who intend to enter the area of occult studies or the spiritual sciences must be careful about implanting any strong belief patterns into their mind. You must be free of any self-induced belief patterns if you are to work in these fields with any hope of success. For the average person who does not intend to become a professional occultist, a strongly implanted belief that they will not accept any negativity from others will do well in giving them protection from everyday negativity and common psychic attack.

The particular belief pattern to be implanted in the mind is a matter of individual choice. A few sample belief patterns will be given below, as well as some instructions on the best matter of implanting. In discussing these belief patterns with a client, the client made a comment that I feel is worth repeating. He said, "Implanting a belief pattern is done in exactly the same manner as programming computer, except that there are no trial runs.

DEFENSE AGAINST COMMON PSYCHIC ATTACK

All of the debugging must be completed before the program is loaded into the computer." Those who are familiar with affirmations will immediately recognize that a belief pattern is actually an affirmation (or vice versa). Belief patterns must be developed in the same way that affirmations are developed by using only positive images. To assist you in developing belief patterns for your own use, some guidelines for forming them are given.

First - There must be no negative statements

Second - Every statement must be as positive as it may be made

Third - The belief pattern must be as short as possible

Fourth - The entire belief pattern must be without any exceptions - it must cover all cases

Fifth - The entire belief pattern must be accepted as completely true by the conscious mind of the person using it

Sixth - The person using the belief pattern must feel that using the belief pattern will bring about a better life, or a bring a better condition into there life

These guidelines are almost self-explanatory. All of the statements in the belief must be positive because the subconscious mind will accept a positive statement over a negative statement. When faced with a new program that contains both positive and negative statements, the subconscious mind will attempt to resolve the conflicts between them before it will accept the program and act on it. Usually the conflicting statements cannot be resolved, so the subconscious mind discards or ignores the entire program.

This also occurs when a belief pattern has emotions or special cases within it. The subconscious mind will attempt to fit the exceptions and special cases in the belief pattern into its experience, and attempt to resolve them before it will act on the belief. This usually results in discarding the entire belief pattern. The individual must find the entire belief pattern to be acceptable and true within their conscious mind. If the conscious mind cannot accept the belief as true, there is

PSYCHIC ATTACK

probably an element in the subconscious mind that does not agree with it. This may cause the subconscious mind to entirely reject the new belief pattern. The subconscious mind is motivated by what it perceives as rewards. Unless the subconscious mind can perceive the possibility of a reward for it within the new belief pattern, it will not accept it.

Beyond these considerations, there is another part of implanting a belief that it which is important, but rarely discussed. You should have a private discussion with yourself before you begin to implant any belief pattern, or begin to use an affirmation. The discussion should dwell on the importance of implanting the belief pattern, and what the benefits of implanting it will be. This discussion should be done with sincerity and complete honesty. You should also listen to and discuss any objections that you might find within your mind. These objections must be removed from your mind, at least from your conscious mind, before you attempt to implant the new belief pattern.

Should you find an objection you are not able to overcome or explain, you must take some time to think about it and attempt to gather arguments that might explain it. What you're doing is actually opening a discussion with your subconscious mind concerning the belief pattern you wish to use. Only after you have held this discussion with yourself, and have overcome all of the objections of your subconscious mind, are you ready to make the real decision to use the new belief pattern. Once you make this decision, after having discussed it with yourself in this way, you will find your subconscious mind will accept the new belief pattern more quickly and effectively than it otherwise would.

To implant any belief pattern it is necessary you enter into the relaxed twilight state between wakefulness and sleep with the new belief pattern repeating firmly in your mind. Play it over and over again like a mantra. To do this correctly you should memorize the new belief pattern before you attempt to use it. Then retire for the night about a half an hour early for two or three nights, and consciously relax yourself, while you repeat the new belief pattern in your mind. Repeat it over and over again until you lose consciousness and go off to sleep.

DEFENSE AGAINST COMMON PSYCHIC ATTACK

Following this two or three day effort you should retire at your regular time and simply repeat the new belief pattern over and over again as you relax and fall asleep. You must continue this process for at least two or three weeks to ensure the new belief pattern is firmly placed into your subconscious mind.

Once the new belief pattern is firmly placed into your subconscious mind you will begin operating on it. It is important you continue to repeat the new belief pattern as you go to sleep for at least a week or two, even after you realize you are operating on it. This ensures it will become a permanent part of your subconscious programming. Once you consciously notice that you are consistently operating on the new belief pattern, you can mark that day, as being one week from the time you will stop repeating it to yourself as you fall asleep. This whole process can take from three or four weeks to as much as four to six months. Here, as in all other things, patience is certainly a virtue.

The method by which any belief pattern is accepted into the subconscious mind is as follows.

First - The existence of the belief pattern is noticed, and the subconscious mind attempts to find any experiences in the experiential memory, which may mitigate again the belief pattern having benefit to the person. The relative utility of the new program, the past experiential memories and their associated belief patterns, are compared in terms of what we shall call pain to the organism, both physical and nonphysical. In each comparison, the experiential memory and the belief patterns are weighing in terms of pain. Whichever causes the most pain will eventually be discarded.

When a new belief pattern is inserted into the mind at a time when the organism is in pain, and when the new belief pattern will end the pain, it is much more quickly accepted and acted upon. This was the case with George in his argument with Ethel. His subconscious mind rapidly accepted his conscious decision to, "Not take it any more." As it saw this new belief pattern was a way to avoid immediate pain. The later circumstances of the week confirmed him in this decision, and completely sealed him off from Ethel's negative thoughts.

PSYCHIC ATTACK

Once the weighing in terms of pain is completed, the new belief pattern will be conditionally accepted. It is now compared to all the other belief patterns within the memory, to determine just how this new belief pattern will fit in. There must be a degree of harmonization between this new belief pattern and all of the other beliefs. Until this harmonization is arrived at, the new belief will be used only in those areas in which it does not interfere with other beliefs, or in areas in which it is already harmonized. This process can be recognized in the case of George, who could not completely harmonizes the belief that he did not have to take anything from Ethel with his belief that his parents were his primary authority figures.

George accepted less negativity from his parents after he had his talk with his father, because the result of the talk was that George saw his father as less of an authority figure than he had formally believed he was. He was unable to reject his belief his parents were authority figures, but by reducing their status in his mind, he was able to reduce the negativity he accepted from them.

From the above we can understand our beliefs are constantly being changed and modified by the circumstances of our daily life. While we accept our primary programs at an early age, these programs are always in the process of being changed and modified by experiences that life provides for us. To some extent, we might say the modification of our programs is one of the reasons for our incarnation. We can also say that understanding our programs, and developing correct ones, is the actual nature of karma. Both of these statements are partially correct but not wholly true. This is why many people say we pick our incarnation, and all the many tests and lessons it will bring to us.

Once a belief pattern is harmonized with all the existing belief patterns and programs within our subconscious mind, it will be used in any and all situations in which it can be applied. Unless there is an immediate and urgent need to accept the new belief pattern, the subconscious mind will work on harmonizing the new belief with other beliefs only when it is free to do so. This is why it is necessary to continue the

DEFENSE AGAINST COMMON PSYCHIC ATTACK

repetition of the new belief program until it has been completely harmonized. For the subconscious mind, pain is in the NOW. The memories of pain are in the experiential memory in the form of emotional energy applied to those experiences in which pain was received. In a state of sleep, the subconscious mind attempts to discharge emotional energy stored in the experiential memory through the process of harmonizing the experiences with the belief memory. When the subconscious mind can make some kind of connection between the two, usually an irrational connection, the energy can be discharged. If the subconscious mind is not able to make some kind of connection through which the energy may be discharge, it may send the energy through to the conscious mind in the form of a puzzling dream or a repetitive irrational thought.

Once this process is understood, the motto over the gate entrance at the Oracle of Delphi becomes obvious. The motto was, "Man know thyself and thou shall know the gods and all creation."

Until a person has rid himself of all belief structure that has the effect of inhibiting the programming of new beliefs, and has discharged all of the emotional energy stored in his experiential memory, he is unable to enter temporary belief programs. These are programs that he can run on a trial basis to accomplish a certain goal he might be interested in achieving. So long as any individual has a number of negative belief patterns within himself, he is unable to use his mind in any creative manner.

The Seth book, The Nature Of Personal Reality, (copyright 1974 by Jane Roberts, published by Prentice Hall Englewood Cliffs New Jersey) explains this whole subject from another but nonconflicting point of view. Attaining this complete freedom from belief structures is only one of the goals of true spiritual training.

Most magical or religious training is actually the implantation of different, usually culturally divergent, but equally rigid, belief structures. As many of the more vicious means of inciting psychic attack are through the magical efforts of those who have implanted these rigid belief structures within themselves,

PSYCHIC ATTACK

we will discuss this process in detail in a later chapter.

Once the method of implantation of the new belief structure is understood, the next tasks task is to write out the new belief that it is desired to implant within yourself. Considering the rules for the new belief structures we read previously, we might prepare a new belief to be implanted into the subconscious mind along one of the following lines.

The mercy and power of Jesus Christ now frees me from all negativity from every source

Through the grace of God, I am no longer the recipient of any negative influences

The need to accept negative or detrimental influences from any source whatsoever has ended. They need no longer affect me in any way

Through the power of the Christ of God within me I am now protected from all negative and harmful spiritual influences from any and every source

Through the power of Jesus Christ, my Savior and Redeemer I am now free from all influences which work against his will in my life

All non-physical influences that are detrimental to my well being, physically, mentally, or spiritually, no longer affect me

Through the power of the divine within me I now realize that I am completely protected from the effects of any and all negative influences that may be sent to me, or which might be near to me, from any source what so ever.

Any of the above belief patterns can be used with equal effect. You should choose the one that is most appealing to you. Then you should use the same one until you can see that you are no longer receiving negativity from any source whatsoever. Then continue to use it for at least another week, as previously mentioned.

For those who are in the position of receiving a continual negative bombardment from a mate, parent, or other close associate, the knowledge that you no longer must receive the pain of the attack can come up from your subconscious mind

DEFENSE AGAINST COMMON PSYCHIC ATTACK

itself as a sigh of relief. Once this new belief program is established, the individual will be protected from common psychic attack. This protection will last them the remainder of their lifetime.

In addition to implanting a belief pattern as a defense against common psychic attack, there is a great deal of protection from psychic attack which are to be found in the full, total, and unconditional acceptance of a religious faith. You choose, as a spirit, the religious faith into which you are to be born. This is so regardless of what part the religious faith is to play in your life. The religious faith, or lack of religious faith, which is found in your home for the first four or five years of your life, becomes the faith that is most completely and implicitly accepted by the subconscious mind as being true.

Only when this religious faith is gradually detangled from their subconscious mind, and removed completely from the behavior pattern of the individual, is it possible for them to live and act in full harmony with divine law. This is not work to be done by oneself, no matter how appealing it may be it may seem to be to the novice.

It is more important to realize that the religious faith that you learned at your mother's knee is the one that is the surest bedrock for success in protecting you against psychic attack of all kinds. By understanding, the importance of this faith in your life it is possible to gain a great deal of protection from psychic attack of all kinds by simply living a life that is in harmony with the tenets of that faith. These tenets are usually simple and not difficult to live by.

If you wish to protect yourself through religion, it is not difficult to do. All religions consider their Godhead as the source of absolute perfection, physically and spiritually. By living a life which is in accordance with the beliefs of the religion to which you were exposed in your childhood, and by making a daily prayer to the Godhead of that religion for protection from spiritual negativity, the active protection of that religion will slowly become a part of your life, so long as your life matches the demands made by that religious practice.

All religions are structured belief systems. Any miracles

PSYCHIC ATTACK

performed through the agency of the structured belief system are performed through the agency of the individual who performs them, and their contact with their own inherent divinity. This is not a popular view of miracles but it is a spiritually correct view of them. Those who have heard it often misunderstand this view of miracles. Few men understand man and his nature, and fewer still have even the least idea of the true nature of either God or divinity. This is why spiritual training always begins with the student beginning to grasp some idea of himself as a being on this Earth.

There is one difficulty with programming a religious belief system onto oneself as a means of protection from spiritual negativity. The difficulty is that religions, being human organizations, change over time. Changes of the religion structure may cause the individual to lose faith with their religion. When an individual really loses faith with their religion, they repudiate it completely, both consciously and subconsciously. This change in the basic religious belief system is always traumatic to the subconscious, as there is a void left which is not easy to fill. Occasionally this change is brought about through the religion revising its doctrine. Until the new doctrine is completely accepted as a belief system by the subconscious mind of the believer, they may find they are open to psychic attack.

As an example of this change, we can cite the changes that occurred within the Roman Catholic Church following the Vatican II conference. Although the abolition of the Latin Trinitarian mass was not required by that conference, it was soon almost universally eliminated. Because of the change to the vernacular mass, there was an exodus of both communicants and religious from the Roman Catholic Church. There was also a substantial increase in the number of communicating Roman Catholics who were the victims of psychic attack. Some of these communicants left the church because of their loss of faith in the ability of the Godhead of the Roman Catholic Church to continue to offer them either psychic or material protection.

The change from the Latin to the vernacular mass also had the effect of adding a large number of former Catholics to those

DEFENSE AGAINST COMMON PSYCHIC ATTACK

who were drawn into the occult and mystical boom in the mid-1960s. Those who were disenchanted by the loss of their religion also swelled the ranks of cults and fringe religious groups at that time. It is a fact that most of those who join the so-called witchcraft explosion between 1965 and 1975 were either former members of the Roman Catholic or Jewish religious.

One of the strongest belief patterns in our society, so strong as to be completely impregnated in every person who passes through our public school system, is a belief that the rational mind and the scientific method are the only means of learning, thinking, or understanding. Current scientific thought repudiates anything that is not subject to rational analysis or objective measurement. One of the criterions of scientific methodology is that something must be comprehensible and rationally explainable through some form of objective measurement and experimental testing. Scientific rational methodology therefore must refute or deny the existence of any nonphysical forces. Knowing this, I have always puzzled over the fact that the American Association For The Advancement Of Science accepts this, yet they allow both psychologists and parapsychologists into their ranks.

Rational science is another structured belief system, and has no more basis in the true reality than any other. The full subconscious acceptance of rational science by any individual implies that they cannot be harmed by any nonphysical force, as they are not accepted as being real. That the scientific belief system does not actually offer any protection against the forces of the spiritual universe is obvious to anyone who has met with an assortment of those who are professional scientists.

University professors, scientists, semi professional skeptics of the unseen world, and all others really accept negativity directed at them by others, regardless of the beliefs of their conscious minds. Their subconscious minds may be forced, through the programming of their professional education, to treat a spiritual universe as unreality. Their subconscious mind, which lives in this universe, is well aware that the spiritual universe exists. Among scientifically trained men the members

PSYCHIC ATTACK

of the medical profession seem to be the most susceptible to the results of negativity, whether the negativity is self-induced or brought to the to them from the negative thoughts of others.

Those who are so embedded in a materialistic philosophy they are unable to see there may be realms of being of which they are unaware, are suffering from a peculiarity of the development of their personal identity. Although this is an accepted form of behavior in our society today, it is nonetheless detrimental to the complete unfoldment of the natural potential of the human being. In time, all of these individuals will likely learn the truth, but it may require a lifetime for them to do so.

In a later chapter we will see the lack of belief in a magical system will not protect an individual from suffering the ill effects of negative magic directed to them through that system. In the same manner, the lack of belief in the ability of the negative influence of common psychic attack to harm one is no protection at all against becoming a recipient of its evil. Negativity is the cause of much human pain and suffering. It is the greatest source of misery on this Earth. No one needs to live their life in negativity, whether it is self generated or directed to them by another.

In the next chapter, we shall explore the nature of psychic attack when it is directed by the deliberate action of the conscious mind. This is more in the area of deliberate cursing, which is always a conscious and deliberate psychic attack.

4

DELIBERATE PSYCHIC ATTACK

Deliberate psychic attack is a focusing of thoughts from the mind of one person into the sub conscious mind and nonphysical body of another. It is accomplished by the action of the conscious mind of the person transmitting the thoughts. When the attack is made to control the individual to whom the thoughts are directed, regardless of the reasons for such control, this psychic attack is an act of moral malpractice, more commonly referred too as black magic. Deliberate psychic attack is usually made to control another person. This includes such consciously directed negative thoughts as those we saw flow from George to Ethel. It includes the conscious projection of thoughts of jealousy, envy, greed, lust, and hate. It also includes the attempt of a parent to bend the will of a child to the will of the parent. The practice of telepathy for the purpose of communication from one person to another is a positive use of this same faculty.

When the individual transmitting conscious thoughts has gained the cooperation of their subconscious mind in the transmission of the particular thoughts they are attempting to send, they are more often successful. When this cooperation is present, the transmission of thought is fueled by the emotions

PSYCHIC ATTACK

present in the subconscious mind and of the sender, directed to its target under the control of the will. This assures the thought will be directed outward to the person who is the chosen recipient for the thought.

When the individual transmitting the thought has not gained the cooperation of their subconscious mind, the thoughts will still be powered by the emotional energy of the subconscious mind, but there may be belief patterns within the sender's mind that prevent or inhibit the release of the full emotional energies outward from them and into the subconscious mind, or emotional body, of the recipient. In this case, the negativity of the thought, which is restricted from being transmitted by the belief patterns of the subconscious mind, will fall back on the person who is making the psychic attack. Occasionally, because of deliberate psychic attack on another person, the attacker will suffer pangs of guilt or remorse for having made the attack. This is a sign there is within the person who launched the attack a belief pattern that inhibits them from attacking others. Some times the attacker may assume the intended victim of the attack is attacking them. At the very least, it shows the attacking individual does not have the cooperation of their subconscious mind in making the attack.

The ability to direct one's thoughts to others, for any reason, is dependent upon at least two factors.

First - The degree of harmonization that exist between the conscious and subconscious minds of the person who is directing their thoughts

Secondly - Upon the spiritual qualities of the individual

Harmonization between the conscious and subconscious mind is the first necessity. This is accomplished through mental and other developmental exercises which can have taken place either in the present incarnation or a previous one. These exercises form the basis for true spiritual training, and their correct completion means the individual so trained in any given incarnation will have made a certain amount of progress on the spiritual path.

True spiritual power always results from true spiritual

DELIBERATE PSYCHIC ATTACK

progress, but spiritual progress is usually long and slow, taking several lifetimes to complete. Religious training is always oriented to the present lifetime, and programs the conscious and sub conscious minds of every member of the religious practice with the doctrine of the religion, while urging them to make some moral progress in their present life.

One of the problems with knowing about the process of reincarnation is that those who know about it may decide to postpone or delay their spiritual growth. When a person feels they have an unlimited amount of time to complete a task, they are unlikely to feel any sense of urgency about beginning the task. This results in an interrupted journey of spiritual progress.

This also reveals there are a number of people who have developed internal harmony in the past existence and who have the ability to make things happen, but who have made only a slight improvement in their moral nature. This usually results in the individual spending a lifetime in the successful control of other incarnate human beings. This control is usually attained through delivered psychic attack of some kind. These individuals will probably spend lifetimes in which they will pay the moral debts they have incurred. It is always better to develop the moral nature than to simply seek spiritual power.

The whole question of spiritual power is one that is often debated by those who have only a vague idea of what it is. I know an asthmatic senior citizen who spends a great deal of time sitting in front of her house repeating over and over again, "All of the power in the universe is available to me and is healing me." She believes that this mantra is helping her in her daily life, and that it is carrying her over fatal physical condition. Her belief makes it as true as her belief will allow it to be. This is one example of spiritual power.

I once met a person who had to train themselves to refrain from saying certain words and phrases, which were commonly used by his family. When he said those words as a young man, the material called for would appear. As an example, he would not exclaim, "Bullshit," under any circumstances, as it resulted in a physical mass which is both difficult to explain and hard to clean up. This is an example of spiritual power of a different,

PSYCHIC ATTACK

and often distressing, kind.

Moral nature is another thing altogether. It is living your life in harmony with the will of your divine nature. The accomplishment of this difficult task in any one lifetime makes it easier to accomplish in any future lifetime. This is a first step to true spiritual development, as from this point on, everything the individual requires will be given to them as a necessity. In other words, once a human soul, incarnate on the earth, is able to manifest his divine nature on the earth, it will no longer find it necessary to manifest its human personality.

This is considerably more difficult in practice than in theory. It is, in fact, the goal of all true spiritual training. This accomplishment gives to the individual who makes it, all of the spiritual power they require to accomplish whatever destiny they have chosen to accomplish as a result of their incarnation on the earth. Once a person is manifesting their divine nature, no further exercises or training are required.

We have seen that the transmission of thoughts from one person to another is dependent upon the belief structure of the subconscious mind. Sometimes, the implantation of a belief structure into the subconscious mind gives a person the right to exert influence on others. This can act to expedite the individual's ability to transmit thoughts. As an example of these belief structures, there exist the idea that they had the right to control their mates, the idea of the parent that they have the right to control their adult child, etc. None of these belief patterns are correct from a divine viewpoint.

If the right to control is present in the subconscious mind of the sender, it is only necessary for the emotion of the sender to be able to overpower the resistance that it will find within the spiritual body of the recipient of the thought. The sender of the thought will either have the power to penetrate the conscious mind of the recipient because of their superior power, or they will have to be satisfied with lodging their thought in the fog of the subconscious mind of the recipient. When a thought is lost in the mental fog that surrounds most people, it will usually be confused with the reverie thoughts that form the normal background of internal conversation within the mind of the

DELIBERATE PSYCHIC ATTACK

average person.

~§~

This same effect is found in those who influence others only with the power of their subconscious mind. The act of the transmission of Malochia is a good example. The relative power of each transmission is determined by the emotional energy that the sender transmits at each occurrence. Some occasions call for a greater release of emotional energy than others. The transmitter might send Malochia that will immediately manifest as burning eyes, a headache, body aches and pains, etc. Other times, the transmission may be of lower energy, and it may be some time before any affliction is felt.

Those who have developed a great deal of so-called spiritual power and have not developed their moral sense can do a great deal of evil in this world through their directed negativity to others. These people often rise rapidly in the world, literally on the bodies of their victims. At some point in their life, they lose their place and usually end their life immersed in self-pity.

Unless a person's mind has been close to the acceptance of negativity from external sources, they are open to whatever negative influences may come within their range. Even if the mind of the person has been closed to the acceptance of external negative influence, it may still, in some circumstances, be overpowered by a powerful individual transmitting negative influence under the control of their conscious mind. The relative spiritual power of the two individuals, and the relative degree of harmonization between their conscious and subconscious minds, becomes the determining factor. Regardless of the degree of harmonization, the conscious transmitter of negativity must always be possessed of sufficient spiritual power to override the inner defenses of their intended recipient.

From the above description, we can begin to see the manner in which the thoughts of the conscious mind are sent out, as in the transmission of a magic spell. Almost all the popular magic spells rely for their efforts on deliberate and conscious psychic attack. They are almost all performed to

PSYCHIC ATTACK

control the actions or thoughts of another human being. As these spells are designed to bring gratification to the animal nature of the person performing them, they are all under the domain of moral malpractice, or black magic.

To make it clear as to what kind of spells I'm referring to, I will list the titles of some spells from a reasonably modern spell book.

To break up a love affair
To bring pressure to bear on an enemy
To heal an unhappy marriage
To arouse jealousy
To win the love of a man
To gain power over others

It should be obvious these spells are not designed to bring the user into a closer relationship with their creator.

None of these, or any other magic spell, are ever performed by accident. The individual performing any magic spell does so deliberately. They perform the spell with all of the attention their conscious mind is able to bring to bear. Within themselves, they are agreed, to the extent they are in harmony with themselves, that they can and should perform the magical operation they are about to undertake.

We must note this says nothing about their expectations for success. Any belief patterns within the subconscious mind that would expedite or inhibit the performance of the spell, or the relative spiritual power of the individuals concerned, may or may not be available to obtain successful results from the spell. Yet, despite this, there is present in the conscious mind an intention to gain some end through the performance of the spell. It is no more possible to perform a magical spell without there being a conscious thought that is the result of the individuals free will than is possible to perform any other voluntary action on accidental basis, such as driving an automobile or skydiving.

The particular spell the person has chosen to use to obtain

DELIBERATE PSYCHIC ATTACK

the effect they desire becomes, in its action, a belief structure to them. The spell may be addressed to a deity, to God, to a spirit, to a saint, or to any force, they consider external to themselves. The spell may be mechanistic in its effect, or it may depend upon the power of the individual to accomplish. However, the spell is supposed to work, it is always a belief pattern for the person using it. If the person has within them a blockage to the acceptance of the belief structure of the spell, the spell will not work for them. This blockage will usually be found within either the belief memory or the experiential memory of the subconscious mind. It may also be found in the experiential memory, where the same ingredients or form of ritual, were used for different purposes.

This is why those who are addicted to the use of magic to solve problems of their daily life try to obtain spells from those they consider good magicians. The reputation of the magician carries over onto the spell they have used. It enhances the belief structure of the spell for the person using it. The reason that magical grimoires are published under the names of supposed masters of magical wisdom should now be obvious.

The ability of the performer of the spell to believe in the effect and validity of the spell has a direct effect on two other constituents of the spell, the emotional energy behind the spell and the effectiveness of the visualization of the results of the spell. The less belief the performer has in the effectiveness of the spell, the more difficult they will find it to be to place emotional energy into the spell to power it. The less the rational mind is convinced the spell will work, the less willing the rational mind will be to power the will to drive the spell to its destination through a clear and unwavering visualization.

Emotional energy calls upon the performers spiritual power on an almost unit for unit basis in those cultures where the emotions are controlled by self-discipline. When the culture gives free rein to emotions, the correlation between emotions and spiritual power is weakened. The ability to release emotions when desired is a learned art, regardless of the culture involved. Orgasmic people have developed this ability, while those who are not usually orgasmic have not.

PSYCHIC ATTACK

Mental discipline, both from training in this life, and as a carryover from prior incarnations, is what holds the visualization of the spell in the minds eye while the spell is being worked. The mental self-discipline of the performer also makes it easier to release the completed spell. Releasing the thought removes it from the mind of the person sending it. This allows it to pass into the mind of the recipient. Mental self-discipline must be reestablished in every lifetime through training, but as with other abilities, which may be carried over from one lifetime to another, the ability to discipline one's mind can become almost an automatic process after several incarnations in which the mind was trained.

We have covered the various facets of the process of magic. We had seen how an individual uses their conscious and subconscious minds to perform what they consider magic through the process we are referring to as direct psychic attack. We have also noted there are a large number of variables which can have an effect on the ability of the specific individual to perform magical spells. We may now define deliberate psychic attack as the shaping of spiritual power through the action of the mind of the performer in accordance with a belief structure. The success of the deliberate psychic attack now relates to the ability of the recipient to receive the attack within their non-physical body, and accept it within their subconscious mind, carry it to their conscious mind, and proceed act upon it.

These factors are not under the control of the performer of the spell, they relate entirely to the recipient. All that any spell caster can do is to shape the power of the spell with as much care as possible, and project the spell with as much intensity as possible. Once that is accomplished, the performer must release the thought from their mind, and literally forget it. The thought being launched, it will either have its effect upon the recipient or it will return to the sender.

When a thought is projected into the non-physical body of a person, the time required for that thought to rise to the conscious mind of the person depends upon the harmonization between the conscious and subconscious minds of the recipient, the belief structure of their subconscious mind as to the possibility of the transmission of thoughts from one person to

DELIBERATE PSYCHIC ATTACK

another, and their resistance to, or agreement with, the particular thought that has been sent to them. Many times the individual receiving the thought will never be aware of the transmission of the thought, even though they begin to act in a manner that agrees with the thought. Almost all the time, should the person who receives the thought become consciously aware of it, they will decide the thought originated in their own mind. The person will usually begin to act on the thought as though they had made the free will decision to do so. Only if they find the conscious thought repugnant, in which case it is unlikely to leave their subconscious mind, will they turn from it and decided against it.

Only in that rare individual, who is able to learn the source of these thoughts which his subconscious mind presents to him for consideration, will the transmission of the thoughts from a source outside of himself be recognized for what it is. Only in these rare cases can the identity of the sender of the thought be revealed. There is no academic way to teach this ability.

When there is a belief pattern in the subconscious mind of the recipient that would either prohibit or inhibit them from acting on the thought, it is even less likely the thought will present itself to their conscious mind. The result of the spell, now the presence of a thought, would be to create a certain amount of confusion within the person's subconscious mind. The subconscious mind would treat the thought through the same method of weighing for pain, as it would treat an implanted belief pattern. As there would be no constant repetition of the thought, and as there would be opposition to the thoughts from existing belief patterns, it would ultimately be rejected. This process has been considered in depth in the chapter on defense against common psychic attack, so we need not go into it here.

This procedure illustrates the necessity of using thought projections in spells that are usually acceptable to the recipient, especially in terms of their familial, cultural, and communal context. Attempting to induce some someone to do something that is against their will is as difficult in magic as it is in hypnosis.

PSYCHIC ATTACK

When a person begins to use magic in the form of psychic attack to control others, they often have a run of beginners luck, in that their first few spells are very successful. Over the course of time, they usually notice a decrease in their ability to perform magic, or cast spells on others. This decrease in magical ability is more common than is generally supposed. Those who are addicted to the use of magical spells to control their fellow man usually attribute this decrease in their ability to the spell itself losing power. They then look for bigger and better spells to use.

The problem is not in their spells it is in them. Almost everyone has a belief pattern within them that discourages them from interfering in the lives of others. As they place energy into doing spell after spell with this interference as their true goal, this belief pattern is activated time and time again. From the activation of this belief pattern, there is generated a fear or guilt within the subconscious mind which builds to the point where it blocks the successful completion of any spell the person tries to use. The only remedy for this connection is to remove all belief patterns and inhibitions from the subconscious mind before beginning to do any spell at all. This requires a great deal of mental discipline and work, in other words training, which ultimately results in true mental clarity. Those who are addicted to the use of magic usually do not take the time and trouble to do this, or even learn of its necessity.

It is possible to program into an individual strong belief patterns that give permission to them to cast spells on others. These permissions blot out or cover up, but do not remove, the belief patterns that prohibit them from interfering in other people's lives. The installation of these strong and effective belief patterns is one of the aims of ordinary occult training and initiation. Having completed a course of ordinary occult training that concludes with initiation into an Occult Lodge, a Fraternity, or Coven, the individual has been inculcated with the belief that they now had been given permission to exert some form of control over the forces of the universe.

Not only does their training certify this, although it may have been as simple as learning to recite the Hebrew alphabet, but they have passed through an impressive initiation that was

DELIBERATE PSYCHIC ATTACK

bestowed by a Grand Master, or a Supreme Noble Leader, an impressive authority figure. This figure has told them, usually in the name of God, that they had been given the authority to control certain forces of the universe, always for the good of all mankind. In addition, they are usually given the implied promise that they do well, and if God, and particularly the authority figure, is pleased by their performance, they will be given further initiations.

The further initiations promise to give them further powers, and so forth. Their state of being, having been changed by the act of initiation, the belief structure that has prohibited them from interfering with others is now covered over with a rationalization that renders it less effective, although it is still in existence.

When a person surrounds himself with others who believe in a way that is different from the social concepts of the culture within which they live, they enter into a subculture. The sub cultural pattern we all live in is changeable, and it is always a subculture, whether we are interested in criminal activity, a political party, an occult group, or social and athletic organization. Every person in every culture is also a member of a subculture that takes most of their time and effort, calls for their emotional and financial support, and provides them with the security of being a member of an approved group of their peers. People accept attention and reinforcement from their subculture; they attain status as a member of the sub cultural group. These all fill the human need people have for acceptance, attention, and status among their peers.

If one can function in the world as a file clerk, it is satisfying to be a leading member of the Ladies Aid Society who is looked at with respect every Sunday in Church. By the same token, if you are a housewife who feels there is nothing really important going on your life, it is very satisfying to your need for importance to be a witch, or even a high priestess, once a month. Filling status needs are never spiritually elevating. The need for recognition and importance among people is of the same order is a need for a chicken to know whom it can peck in its flock, and whom it must allow to peck it. They are social

PSYCHIC ATTACK

classification needs, important, but nothing more.

This need, being attained through some form of recognition in the subculture one decides to enter, is what one may perceive as initiation. They initiation can be as bland as the academic graduation ceremony at which you receive your degree, or it could be as impressive as an initiation into an Occult Lodge or Magical Order, in which everyone is dressed in an impressive manner and the room is draped with impressive symbols. Once you accept this initiation, whatever it is, you are released on parole from certain belief patterns that have kept you from behaving toward your fellow human beings in a certain way. The more the initiation "takes" on a particular person being initiated, the more the subconscious belief patterns are altered by it. Initiation is used in this manner by civil, fraternal, religious, and academic organizations, as well as by occult groups and even by those rare groups that actively seek to promote true spiritual growth.

Less this description of the process of initiation cause one to think badly of the act itself, it will be well the point out that even Jesus Christ had to receive the initiation of baptism at the hands of his cousin, John the Baptist, before he could go forth upon his mission. Those who feel they are above initiation, or who believe they do not need initiation to practice in certain areas, should bear this in mind. Self-initiation and self-spiritual elevation are fantasies of those who feel they are above the earth. No one who incarnates upon this earth is above it, and the earth must always be given its due in every case.

Among those who seek to grow spiritually, initiation is first done to welcome the individual onto the spiritual path. This may be compared to the ceremony of bar mitzvah or the sacrament of first communion. At a latter time, a further initiation is usually performed to mark the person's arrival at a certain place along the path. More information on this subject may be found in the Gospels, Mark 1:4 – 13 and Matthew 3:1 – 17. The real power of initiation is always bestowed by divinity; initiation itself is simply the earthly recognition of that bestowal. This is always the case with all true and valid initiations.

We have reviewed the manner of deliberate psychic attack,

DELIBERATE PSYCHIC ATTACK

both from the standpoint of the attacker and that of the victim. We shall now examine a few cases of deliberate psychic attack so we may understand the difference it presents from the slow grinding pressure of the common psychic attack. They are different, although their treatment may be the same.

EXAMPLES OF DELIBERATE PSYCHIC ATTACK

I personally know all the following examples of deliberate psychic attack, except the experiences of Ms. Diane Fortune, either from my contact with clients in my daily practice, or from my experience as a student in the field. Names have all been changed and the locations modified to avoid the possibility of identification. That they are all actual cases must be stressed, as some of them may seem to border on the realm of fantasy to those who have had no experience in this work.

These cases are presented as pathologies and are not intended to be suggestions for behavior. The only true purpose for magical practice is for the elevation of the human soul through the demonstration of the living presence of the Creator of all things. It cannot be repeated too often that any attempt to control another person through deliberate psychic attack is moral malpractice, regardless of the reason for attempting such control.

Aside from those inevitable rehashing of the details of witchcraft persecutions in the Middle Ages, I know of only one major book in the English language which discusses the

EXAMPLES OF DELIBERATE PSYCHIC ATTACK

problem of psychic attack and its defense. This is the undoubted bestseller of the occult book world, Psychic Self Defense by Ms. Dion Fortune. First published in 1930 it has remained a standard work in the occult field ever sense. It is usually the first book to the novice occult student is required to purchase, regardless of the group that is training them.

Dion Fortune was herself was the victim of psychic attack, and in her book she described the attack as well as the physical and mental trauma which was a result of the attack. She was, as she describes herself in her book, a mental and physical wreck for over a year. She was partially healed by spending time in an occult retreat. Her final healing came about as she received initiation into Occult Lodge that was an offshoot of the famous Order of the Golden Dawn.

As she describes in her book, Dion Fortune was attacked by her employer in a face-to-face confrontation, in which the employer impressed into Dion Fortune's mind the idea that Mrs. Fortune was an incompetent and had no self-confidence. The employer did this deliberately, with malicious intentions. This thought was so impressed into Dion Fortune's mind it caused her not only mental and emotional problems, it also created in her physical lassitude, a complete lack of physical energy, and an inability to function in the world. In effect, the attack by her employer superseded all of Dion Fortune subconscious beliefs to the contrary, forcing her to think and act as though she was indeed an incompetent with no self-confidence.

Dion Fortune pointed out she believed her employer had been trained in some of the occult arts in India. This case is cited to demonstrate that deliberate psychic attack need not be done in an atmosphere of the arcane and the ritualistic. In fact, it may be, and often is, accomplished in the more familiar setting of the home, office, or workplace. This kind of direct and confrontational psychic attack is the same as any other, except that the victim may, at the least, suspect they are being psychically attacked.

This kind of directly confrontational verbal attack is often used in military training units, with the result that the person so attacked is often rendered worthless as a combat soldier,

PSYCHIC ATTACK

although they may still march and parade well enough. Having lost their belief in themselves, and their self confidence, they are unlikely to be able to fire their rifle effectively in a real combat situation, where self confidence and calm self assurance are always required. Unfortunately, this is the kind of training that most armies use today.

Some office workers, usually a small clique in an office, may amuse themselves by telling a coworker they are not looking well. Continuing this over the course of a week or so, they frequently succeed in causing the victim of their malefic attention to become physically ill. This is as evil psychic attack as any other, although it is considerably more common, in my experience.

Another common form of psychic attack is that which is done to promote revenge for a supposedly injury. The following case that I was made aware of as described below, comes from my first years in New York City.

I used to spend weekends sunning myself in a small park near my home. One of the other regular visitors to the park was a middle-aged black lady. She was employed as a maid in one of homes nearby. One afternoon, as the cooler days of fall were approaching, she came over to the bench where a friend and I were sitting. She joined us and proceeded to open herself up to me. She explained that she had been severely reprimanded by her employer for some oversight. She went on to tell us in great detail she was going to take revenge on her employer, describing the proposed revenge in detail. She revealed she was going to work a spell on her employer through the agency of a deity I had never heard of. By the time, she was finished speaking to us, her eyes were flaming, and she was trembling with emotion. She rose suddenly from the bench, and walking to a nearby tree, cut a tree twig from it. She then walked away from us mumbling to her while she turned the twig she held between her fingers. As she reached the path leading from the tree, she suddenly snapped the twig and cast both pieces away. She left the Park with a jaunty step, and without a backward glance. The following Saturday afternoon she was back in the Park. My friend and I were sitting on our usual bench as the lady walked right up to us as

EXAMPLES OF DELIBERATE PSYCHIC ATTACK

pleased as could be. She informed us that her employer had broken his leg, the exact punishment she described to us she was preparing for him.

I am reasonably certain this charming lady had no idea that my friend and I spoke English as we have been speaking another language when she first approached us. Nor did she care what our language shortcomings were, as she was using her one sided conversation with us to build up an emotional charge preparatory to committing the deliberate psychic attack on her employer. The twig, although it possibly had some relationship to the deity she mentioned, became the focal point of the malignant energy of her spell. She transferred this energy to her employer by breaking the twig and released it by casting the pieces aside. Effectively she ordered her employer to break his leg and he did. This was my first introduction to American folk magic.

Another similar case was that of a young woman who was referred to me by her lover. The woman was suffering from acute emotional trauma, frequently breaking into tears for no obvious reason. She worked in an office, and her emotional state was sufficiently bad she was in danger of losing her job. After examining her, it became obvious the woman was the victim of a curse. That the curse originated from a woman who was a total stranger to the victim, was something puzzling to me. I question the young man who brought her to me, while the victim was in another room. The young man was able to identify the sender of the curse as a woman he had kept company with before you met his current friend. I broke the curse on the woman prepared protective charms for both of them. As I expected the woman who had placed the curse found out she has failed to harm the other woman, so she cursed the man. The protection charm operated, and kept the curse from reaching him. The curse she had sent to the man rebounded on her.

This was not the end of the matter, for one fine day, shortly after the man had told me the charm had certain effects, a young lady came to my door and explained she thought she had accidentally placed a curse on herself. She insisted that it

PSYCHIC ATTACK

had happened by accident, through her reading a magical spell the book out loud. I told her it was impossible to curse oneself or anyone else by accident. Because she had a certain feel to her, I asked her if she were not in the habit of cursing her former lovers. At that, she broke down and confessed the whole story. I remove the curse that had rebounded on her, and extracted from her a solemn promise not to curse people again.

There are people who have the moral right to deliberately psychically attack others. These people always use their talent both wisely and carefully, which is why they have the right to influence others in this way. A case of this sort was reported me by the woman who was involved in it. On a very snowy day in New York, with a very heavy snow cover on the ground, she had managed to dig her car out of its parking space after a half an hour's hard work. As she was warming up the engine of her automobile, a man came along plowing out the parking lot with his truck. He blocked off her car with three-foot high wall of snow. The young woman was quite distressed, but she sat quietly in her automobile and prayed the man would have as much extra work for himself as he had given her. She then left her automobile and shoveled the way out, clearing it once again. As she was slowly driving out of the parking lot, she noticed the snowplow truck had run into a ditch that ran along the road on one side of the parking lot. His truck was now stuck in the snow, and as she passed it, she noticed he was shoveling it free. This young lady had the moral authority to influence other people and she used it following the maxim of the martial arts, using as little force as was required to remedy the situation.

Some cases of deliberate psychic attack exceed the realms of decency and good taste, to the point they should not be reported in published works. Others exceed the belief of those who cannot accept that such things can be done through a nonphysical agency. Whenever a person holds a thought within their mind that can be fed by the thought of another person, they are liable to become the victim of psychic attack solely because the thought they hold can be fed by the malefic energy of another. This makes it possible for the negatively inclined

EXAMPLES OF DELIBERATE PSYCHIC ATTACK

magician to dominate the supposedly unwilling victim. The victim has a similar thought or inclination within their mind that allows the impulse of domination to find a comfortable and compatible home.

A woman living in the coal country of Pennsylvania was the recipient of a slight degree of attention through a man, who had, to her, excellent prospects in life. She decided that if she were to become his wife she would be surrounded with the style of life she wanted, which was what she had seen only movies and magazines. As the woman encouraged the man's attention, she also discussed the situation with her mother and an aunt. They all approved the proposed match. The woman, her mother and aunt, visited a local Hexenmeister, who gave them a surefire spell to win the young man's affection. The young man was attending Columbia University in New York City. On his return to his hometown, he had the occasion to have dinner with the young woman and her family. There were ingredients of the spell added to the food of the dinner. The family had done this following the counsel of the Hexenmeister. Unfortunately, for their plans, the young man visited me upon his return to the city with another question entirely. During the course of our discussion, I mentioned to him that a weak spell had been cast upon him, and I broke it in front of him.

He was intrigued that the woman had cast a spell on him, as he had no interest in her. He wrote her at some length breaking off their friendship. After he graduated from the University did not return to live in the rural town where magic of this sort was commonly practiced.

Lest anyone think that this sort of spell is rare, I know a couple who have been reasonably happily married for a number of years where the wife had used the same spell to make the man fall in love with her. I have never mentioned this to the husband, but the wife is aware that I know how they came to be married. The use of love spells is far more common than one would suppose. The most important thing about using them is breaking them after of the person who has cast a spell falls out of love with their victim. To tell people not use love spells is to whistle against the storm. People use them anyway.

PSYCHIC ATTACK

In the first example, the spell did not work because young man had no carnal desire for the young woman in the second case the spell did work because the young man had a carnal desire for the young woman involved.

A man loaned some money to a woman, expecting that the woman would reimburse the loan not only financially but physically. When the financial reimbursement began to return slowly, and there seemed to be no prospect of any physical reimbursement, the man cursed the woman with a great deal of emotional force. The woman, employed as a salesperson the Seventh Avenue fashion markets, saw the man frequently at her place of business. She noticed that her affairs were not prospering, and through a friend was referred to me. In our discussion, a number of problems emerged. The curse the man had placed on her was removed, and she decided to pay back the full amount of money she had borrowed from him as soon as possible, severing her connection to him. This spell worked because it was matched by the woman's desire to get the better of the man. She would like to have avoided paying back the loan at all.

A young man attending college was called daily by his mother during the first few years of his studies. All through this time, he noticed that he was remarkably unsuccessful in his social life. He could not maintain a friendship with any of the young ladies he had met at school. This and other concerns led him to be referred to me for a consultation. In the course of our discussion, I mentioned that his mother had a strong hold on his life, and in fact wanted to be the only woman in his life. He explained, "That's why I can't get a girlfriend."

I agreed with his self-diagnosis and made some suggestions to him as to how he could loosen the cord of her influence. He returned later, mentioned that he was seeing a young lady regularly. He was also considering working away from his hometown, something that he had not previously considered. In this case, because the young man was feeding energy into the connection with his mother, it was impossible to break them apart. It was possible to limit the mental tie to the extent that his mother could no longer work against him, or interfere in his life. The mother had tied her son to her through using some of

EXAMPLES OF DELIBERATE PSYCHIC ATTACK

his baby hair, which she had made into a charm and prayed over every night. There was no question in my mind that this was a deliberate psychic attack on the part of his mother. I did not inform the young man of this, because he would not have been able to accept that his mother was capable of any such a negative act.

A man had gotten into a bar fight and had been severely beaten. His wife used a book of spells to do magic against the winner and get revenge. She kept up her efforts for an entire week, focusing all of her negativity and rage in the direction of the winter the brawl. The following weekend the winner of the previous weeks brawl was badly beaten in another fight at the same bar. The wife of the first victim was triumphant. She proceeded to tell how she had done in the man who had beaten her husband. Unfortunately bar fighters are bar fighters, sometimes they win, and sometimes they lose. The woman's negativity may have contributed to the man's losing but I doubt it was the only cause. This is a case of the person attempting to perform magic, but while she was sure of the outcome, it actually was in doubt.

While she was in high school young lady decided she was in love with a young man. She, like many other young ladies of high school age, considered herself a witch. She decided to do a spell to ensure that her relationship with the young man would continue. Locating a book that gave directions to that effect, she performed a spell. As a grown woman in her early 30s, she came to me with the same boyfriend in the same relationship and still not married to him. She found him in her own words, "Convenient but boring."

She was, at the time, she came to see me, involved in two other sexual relationships, but she could not get rid of the first boyfriend, whom she had once prayed to be with forever. After discussion with her, she decided that the spell she had cast on her high school boyfriend should be released. Under my direction, she released the spell, and within a week, she broke off the long-lasting affair. It is worth noticing that spells of the ego often do not work. Their result is often a feeling of fear or guilt on the part of the person who performed the spell. This

PSYCHIC ATTACK

process was previously mentioned in chapter four.

A woman from a strictly Protestant fundamentalist background was visiting a relative in New York City and there fell in love with a man was quite beyond her in education, culture, and social status. The girl cast a spell to catch the man, a spell that a girlfriend gave her to get her, "one true love." She then allowed herself to be seduced by the man, the only time she was ever along with him. She returned to her home, prepared to hear from him at any time. The man never called or wrote, the woman having passed completely from his mind.

The woman developed a severe guilt complex about doing a spell to catch the man and about allowing herself to be seduced by him, although it would probably be more honest to say that she had seduced him.

She returned to New York City the following year obsessed with her guilt her fears. Her relative who is a client of mine discussed the changes the girl's attitude toward life with me, and I suggested the relatives have a frank discussion with the girl. It developed that the girl thought that she had sold her soul to the devil because of her use of the spell to catch a man. Her relative, who is an intelligent and sensitive person, was able to dissuade the girl from her fears and release her from some of the chains that her background had placed her under. The woman returned to her family less obsessed and despondent than she had been when she arrived to visit her friend.

Occasionally you will find groups of people who seem to have nothing to better to do than to mind other people's business. These groups can cause a great deal of difficulty to those to whom they turn their negative attention. Groups usually tend to work in harmony to a gain a given end, and when there is someone within the group who can actually shape the energy of the group thought, the entire power of the group can be focused on the person who is to be the target of the groups attack. In this rare case, the prayer of the group may have its desired effect on the otherwise unsuspecting victim.

Church groups that have prayer services, particularly those of the more exuberant Protestant Fundamentalist

EXAMPLES OF DELIBERATE PSYCHIC ATTACK

denominations, seem to take great delight in praying to change the ways of those whose behavior does not conform to their standards. This sort of magic is no different than any other form of black magic, except that their deliberate psychic attacks have the sanction of the church group that sponsors it.

The minister of one such Protestant Fundamentalist congregation in the Midwest absconded with a sum of money from the church treasury, and the wife of one of the members of the church. The church group gathered to pray for him at their regular weekly prayer meeting. They spent about two hours praying for him and adjourned. The minister had fled to New York City with the young lady in the cash. Within an hour after the cessation of the midwestern prayer meeting, the minister suffered a fatal heart attack in the restaurant where he had been having dinner with the young lady. The owner of the restaurant was a client of mine, and hearing the woman sobbing, "They prayed him to death," he suggested to her she see me at once.

The next time the congregation was scheduled to gather for prayer the young lady was with me. The force of the congregational prayer was diverted back to the person in the congregation who was directing it. The following Wednesday night lady was also with me, but the prayer was completely divergent and undirected. At my suggestion, the young woman disappeared from sight of the congregation, although the body of the former minister was returned to the care of his murderers.

In this case, the ethics of the situation was not my concern, except to state that murder is never ethical, regardless of the means. The woman was able to make a new life for herself, something she had been attempting to do with the man who had been killed. After the body of the former minister was returned to the church, the praying stopped completely. As the prayer, while it continued, it never again had either focus or direction; I can only assume that the person who had been guiding the energy of the prayer was no longer among those praying.

During the course of the woman's divorce, which occurred

PSYCHIC ATTACK

about three years later, the woman learned one of the members of the prayer group had suffered a nervous breakdown during the second prayer meeting, and had left the church.

There is no difference between a church prayer group and a witch's coven when the intent is malicious. For the most part, modern witches coven usually either work for healing or for money for themselves. For some reason it seems that most of the malefic work they do is directed toward other witches. As some witches covens have members who can actually perform magic, and as most of them have belief patterns, which allow them to believe they can perform magic, the results are often interesting, although they are rarely either harmful or deadly.

A young woman in her early 20s, the daughter of a witch was placed under the wing of a spiritual teacher, at the request of another woman, also a witch. The spiritual teacher was made aware the girl's mother would probably attack him, which occurred as soon as the mother learned the girl's intention.

The mother had an extreme run of bad luck because of her attack. The spiritual teacher had simply set up an elementary safeguard the girl's mother and her companion witches had found impossible to pierce. I watched one of these attacks take place while visiting the teacher. It would seem that no matter what the coven tried to do, it rebounded on their head as soon as it was sent out. Meanwhile the teacher and those of his household were entirely unconcerned, acting as if there was nothing happening, which was exactly the condition from their point of view.

In mid-1960s, the occult was an *in* thing, and the practice of witchcraft became almost a popular religious effort. With all of the activity present, there had to be some reality behind it, no matter how it was concealed. I had the opportunity to meet one of these pop witches in a bookstore. He gave me a long talk, and in the course of it, I mentioned that a woman had cursed him. He said he was aware of it, and that he intended to curse her back. I suggested the best course of action for him was simply to go to nearby St. Patrick's Cathedral and pray for her forgiveness at a statue the Blessed Virgin Mary. Giving

EXAMPLES OF DELIBERATE PSYCHIC ATTACK

me a curt and curious look, he said that he would do so, and that he would give me a call as to the result. About a week later, he called me to say that the woman who cursed him had dropped out of their witchcraft group. He even mentioned he felt he should also leave the group, as he was beginning to feel it would not take him anywhere. I encouraged him in that decision, and about a month later, he called to tell me he had left the group, reverting to a pleasant state of a non-believer.

There is a vast amount of difference in the result of an attack by a trained mind and an attack by the most vicious untrained person. The person who is trained, skilled, and has an understanding of the effects of his efforts, can attack another person psychically without their ever being aware they have been the victims of such an attack. This vastly surpasses simply having a skill; it is true professionalism in the field of magic at its best. The person with this degree of skill is one who never attacks another for the gratification of their ego drives. They are beyond responding to the nature of their animal self. They use their powers for the furtherance of the evolution of humanity as a whole. That their actions are usually not comprehensible to the average person is beyond question. I could list a number of cases of this type, performed by those who were teachers of mine. These cases are interesting in that they there is both an action which is open to the observer, but there is also a long-term result which takes a long time to develop but which may eventually be seen.

A man who was a self-styled spiritual teacher called to visit my teacher during one of his weekly public meetings. The man had recently advertised himself as a spiritual teacher in our local newspapers and had not found a warm reception. He began the discussion with my teacher by explained he recently severed his connection with a prominent Indian Guru, and had decided he should begin teaching on his own. He had come to ask my teacher where he should locate, and how he should attract pupils to himself. Those of us who were students were quite sure our teacher would denounce this pompous ass for the fraud that he was, and sent him packing. Instead our teacher seemed to be warmly receptive to his plans, he congratulated

PSYCHIC ATTACK

the man on his decision, and described in detail a small town in southern France, that he stated would be the best place for him to establish his teaching. He then went on to describe to the man in detail, just how he should go about soliciting for students. Our teacher took a great deal of time with this pseudo-teacher, and the man left obviously pleased and self-satisfied, while the students of my teacher were amazed. At the close of the meeting, we discussed the question among ourselves at some length. We could find no resolution or understanding of our teacher's actions.

The following evening, in a regular private session, our teacher began his remarks by explaining his reply to the man in the following way.

"Is important to understand what one can prevent and what one cannot prevent. The man who visited here yesterday is going to consider himself an enlightened teacher regardless of what he hears from others. No amount of discouragement will keep him from teaching, because he has decided subconsciously that only through teaching will his animal instincts for the trappings of mystery, authority, and power, be gratified. Through instructing him in a certain method of attracting students to himself, and through pointing out a specific location for him to center his teachings, I have at least been able to ensure that there will be a positive result of his teaching. He will draw to himself only those who will benefit from his teaching."

The man followed the advice given him by our teacher, and proceeded according to the plan my teacher had given him. Within a few years, he was successful in his teaching, and had gained a good reputation for his abilities as a teacher and spiritual leader. While most of his students only stayed with him for about three years, before either leaving him for another teacher, or losing interest in spiritual teaching altogether, he did develop a small core group that surrounded him. He passed a large number of students through his school in the years it was open. Occasionally, even now, I hear of someone who had studied with him, or who has heard of him. When I do, it always brings to my mind how I so completely misunderstood my teacher.

EXAMPLES OF DELIBERATE PSYCHIC ATTACK

Lest anyone not recognize the elements of psychic attack present, it was in my teacher's explanation to him. My teacher made following his detailed instructions so appealing to the man there was no chance he would deviate from them in any way. The man found the results of following my teachers instruction so personally satisfying that he joyfully followed them for the rest of his life. He was personally successful in his teaching, his animal nature was pleased, and he eventually died a contented man.

MISCELLANEOUS KINDS OF PSYCHIC ATTACK

In my book, <u>Spiritual Cleansing</u>, I mentioned briefly a number of forms of psychic attack that are far better known in the popular press than they are in real life. Not every psychic phenomenon is a psychic attack. Some of them are simply the result of influences from the nonphysical universe that we do not recognize as normal. That there are unexplained and unknown things in the universe does not mean they are evil.

Psychic attack, regardless of how occurs, is not usually beneficial for its victim. Some rare forms of psychic attack are always classed as being evil. One of these is a total domination of one person by another that I will refer to as psychic takeover. It is one of several kinds of psychic attack known as illicit influence. Psychic takeover is usually accomplished through the projection of thoughts from the attacker to the victim. While in most cases a thought projection is conscious, in some cases it may be subconscious. When the thought projection is subconscious, it could be classified as a common psychic attack, when conscious it is a deliberate psychic attack.

What makes this kind of psychic attack so vicious, despite

MISCELLANEOUS KINDS OF PSYCHIC ATTACK

its relative rarity today, is that is usually used in a family setting, to force a child to care for a parent. It is accomplished by the strong projection of thoughts from the parent to the child, along with the parent verbally making the child feel guilty if they are not attentive to the desires of the parent. Strong thought projections and verbal stress on duty and guilt are what usually lead the child to become dominated by the parent.

While caring for an aging parent may well be a child's responsibility, when the parent rules the life of the child in the process it is definitely an act of moral malpractice. Some of us may be familiar with a case in which an aging parent held an adult child at home, bending the child to the will of the parent and forcing the child to give up hope for a life of its own, becoming practically the parent's slave. These cases are more often found in literature than they are in real life today, but they do still exist. Unfortunately, there is no easy solution to this problem. Any child who falls so much under the influence of their parent as to enslave themselves to the parents, can rarely set itself free. Should they be freed by outside circumstances, the child is often lost, and has neither goal nor direction in their life.

A truly caring parent encourages their child to become a self-supporting adult, taking their places an equal citizen among their peers. When a parent holds a child by their side, refusing to allow them to grow into maturity, they are permanently harming their child. Having a child even though it is an animal act, gives the parent the moral responsibility to raise a child to independent adulthood. When this responsibility is not completed correctly, the parent must ultimately answer to their creator for their neglect.

Psychic takeover is not often found outside of the parent-child relationship. When found it is always a deliberate psychic attack. It is impossible for a person to put as much energy into another person as is required to control them without the attacker realizing what they are doing. It has always seemed to me the psychic takeover between the parent and child is a deliberate psychic attack. To affect psychic takeover, the person who is attempting to gain control must spend hours

PSYCHIC ATTACK

every day directing their thoughts to their victim. They must visualize their victim in the position they wished them to assume, and mentally insist with their willpower that their victim is in that position. Through spending this effort daily, over a long period, the attacker may finally overcome the willpower of their intended victim.

Psychic takeover always requires the expenditure of tremendous amounts of time and effort. It also requires the intended victim be suggestible and passive by nature, or all of the attackers his work is in vain. A person who is strong-willed and active, with activities outside their home, cannot be forced to surrender their personal autonomy to another.

Defense against psychic takeover is relatively simple. As mentioned in Spiritual Cleansing, once the intended victim becomes aware that someone is attempting to influence them, taking simple cleansing precautions will frustrate the attacker. For example, placing a glass of water by the head of your bed will make it virtually impossible for anyone to transmit thoughts to you while you sleep. Praying for protection, every day will keep you safe from the ordinary demanding thoughts of others. For the most part, the desires of people to control others are rarely if ever satisfied. Even the most tightly controlled person response first to the desires of their free will.

Another form of taking command of a person is known as theft of the soul, although that is not what it is at all. Theft of the soul is actually a magical attack upon individual self-guidance abilities. When the attack is successful, the victim becomes accident-prone. This blocks the victims mnemonic and observation abilities, they become weak willed, and lethargic. They may lethargically accept whatever position they are placed into. After reaching this point they can literally be turned into slaves without any difficulty, often by simply taking them by the hand and leading them away.

From the description of the condition, the relative rarity of the attack can be assessed. It is almost never successfully performed, although several spells for performing it are available. In my experience, which is to say from the one case I have actually seen where the theft of the soul was

MISCELLANEOUS KINDS OF PSYCHIC ATTACK

successfully performed, is much more difficult to place this psychic attacks upon the victim then it is to remove it from them. I have seen a few other cases where this work had reportedly been done but in those cases the victims was either willingly attaching themselves to the dominator, or was the victim of other work. The field of psychology has a number of techniques that are more useful for making a person into a willing and permanent follower than has the art of magic.

Psychic vampirism is another and more common form of psychic attack. Usually the vampirism is entirely subconscious on the part of the attacker. Conscious psychic vampirism is at least as rare as conscious malochia. It is unlikely you will ever meet anyone who can consciously do either.

Sub conscious psychic vampirism is occasionally found in older people, especially those who are ill, and full of self-pity. It can be prevented by simply having the elderly person sleep with a glass of water at the head of their bed. Older people usually draw energy from those of their own household. Anyone who begins to feel tired or sleepy, or feel they are losing vital energy around others, should take precautions against psychic vampirism. Waking frequently with the feeling of having not slept is an occasional thing with all of us. Should it repeat after two over two or three nights it becomes necessary to take precautions against psychic vampirism. There are a number of possible causes, but they will all be remedied by the remedies against psychic vampirism mentioned in the chapter on protection while asleep in Spiritual Cleansing. The first action is to always have a glass of water set out by the head of your bed when you're sleeping. The water should be changed every day on awakening.

Psychic attacks by spirits of the dead are another feature of novels and thrillers. If these attacks were as common in fact is in movies and novels, there would be a greater demand for the services of spiritual workers. Energy loss or vitality drain from spirits is common, but an attack by the spirit of the dead is very rare.

The real reason for the rarity of these attacks is that spirits lose vital energy in attacking the living. Most spirits lose all of

PSYCHIC ATTACK

their vital energy in the first attack. The attacking spirit, regardless of who or what, has a very limited amount of energy to deal with. The spirit is usually either aware of this, or senses it. They try to use all of their energy in their first attack. Most spirits cannot regain energy after they lose it; so one attack is all they ever managed. Any attack by a spirit of the human dead is not usually successful.

Some spirits will spend time with people they believe "owe them," attempting to drain energy from them. Sometimes they are successful; in most times they are not. The symptoms of this are tiredness, thoughts of, or even a sense of, the deceased being with you, and often difficult and tiring sleep. In rare cases the spirit of the dead; usually a former member of the family, will draw on, or attempt to drain energy from, someone who is still living. This is a form of conscious psychic attack on the part of the spirit. They may be attempting to cause the death of the person they are drawing on. The victim thinking about the departed person more frequently than they normally would as well as thinking about their own death identifies this serious problem.

In many cases the victim begins to feel weak, constantly tired, and without energy of their own. In time, they may develop a serious illness. Aside from seeing a physician, the remedy for this problem is consultation with a spiritual practitioner. The first aid suggestions in Spiritual Cleansing should be taken immediately. Praying for the repose of the soul of the departed is occasionally effective, but a consultation with a spiritual practitioner concerning the problem is recommended.

Psychic attacks by demons, ghouls, monsters, and so forth, are always a product of the individual's subconscious. These require consultation with a psychologist more frequently than a consultation with a spiritual practitioner. Once a person is able to accept themselves with all of their faults and shortcomings exposed, they no longer have such attacks. The first question to ask yourself when you think that you are the victim of such an attack is why the demon or ghoul would attack you. If you can find no real purpose would be served by such an attack, it is probably not happening.

MISCELLANEOUS KINDS OF PSYCHIC ATTACK

Demons, ghouls, and monsters of various kinds exist only as thought forms. These fantasies of the mind are fed by the emotional energy of those who believe in them. Those who suffer from guilt, fear, and suppressed self-hate, often call up images of this kind, which are all too frequently represented in the popular press. To some extent, the demons and other figments of their imagination serve a purpose for the deluded person's mental stability. In order that they regain real mental stability, they need to enter into a course of mental treatment conducted by a metal health professional, psychologist, or psychiatrist.

Possession by spirits and even deities is a real enough phenomena, but they are simply a phenomenal. Possession may be very beneficial for some people. For other people, possession may have negative effects. In no case should anyone engage in such things as mediumship or channeling unless they are under the control of the legitimate priests of a religion in which possession is a part of their religious practice. I have seen a medium that became possessed at a religious ceremony, severely dressed down by the priest for allowing the possession. The first thing a true medium is taught is how to avoid an unwanted possession. In almost all situations, the person becomes possessed by a part of themselves. This happens whether they are passing through an ancestor, a great teacher, or a deity. It might be well the point out here that those who have teachers who pass through mediums have them because they have not yet earned the right to a living spiritual teacher. True spiritual teachers are living human beings who will speak your language and who will communicate with you face-to-face.

Possession by demons and devils is always a mental pathology. Those who have experienced this phenomenon should always see a psychologist who is in their religious practice, either before or following their exorcism. Once a mental difficulty is cleared up, they will never have difficulty with possession again. It is my belief that only priests, ministers and rabbis, members of the clergy, should receive training as mental health workers. Obviously, this is not a

PSYCHIC ATTACK

socially accepted belief, but in my experience, it would make the road back to sanity easier for those who have departed from their childhood religious belief structure.

A clergyman of the childhood faith of the victim should always do an exorcism. Those who are not raising religious homes are almost never possessed by anything except their own guilt and fears. In these cases, the fact that a mental pathology is present is obvious, and psychiatric assistance is immediately applied.

Possession is never a psychic attack, it is simply possession, regardless of who or what the possessing entity claims to be. Most possessing entities that are not deities claim all sorts of wonderful things for themselves. Their claims are false, as can be demonstrated by putting them to the test.

In the Middle Ages there were tales of attacks by sexual demons. Incubus and succubus entered dreams to torment chaste and pious monks, priests, and nuns, while they slept. These so-called dream attacks are emotional reactions to sexual dreams; they are not psychic attacks at all. Should a person report being attacked by such demons in their sleep they had best seek qualified mental health care. It is never been my experience, or that of any other spiritual practitioner whom I know, that such dreams have any basis except sexual frustrations within the individual. These so-called attacks usually occur to those who have guilt concerning their sexuality, and have no regular sexual outlet. While these teams can be quite disturbing, even traumatic, they are generated internally.

When a person is projecting thoughts of lust on another person, the thoughts are not usually received identified with their originator. This is especially true if the originator is not desired as a sexual partner, or not known to the recipient. Sexual thoughts are usually modified in the mind of the receptive to correlate to someone the receptor desire sexually. Projecting lustful thoughts to another person is a waste of time if the person does not respond to you physically. Sending them lustful thoughts of you will usually only make them more open to someone else. This is obviously not your goal, so projecting these thoughts does more harm than good.

MISCELLANEOUS KINDS OF PSYCHIC ATTACK

The most common dream that a human being has are sexual dreams. Fortunately, we do not remember these dreams. According to a scientific study of dreams, the average person has six or eight sexual dreams each night. It would be difficult to clear our minds for the day's affairs if we had these dreams lingering in our conscious mind. These dreams usually have no basis in reality except for the necessity of the animal part of the human being for sexual release. Despite any thoughts to the contrary, these are not psychic attacks. In a few, very rare, instances sexual dreams can relate to spirit influence. The only case I have seen of this influence was reported to me by an elderly woman who visited me to ask about it. Her former husband, who was reliving with her the sexual escapades of their youth, was visiting her in her sleep.

Another thriller mentioned frequently in novels and fictional accounts of magical practice is murder by magic. It is even reported occasionally in the press. This is a very rare phenomenon, as it may be accomplished only by a person who has well-developed powerful magical abilities, and who is without moral sense. While magical murders do occur, they are a very rare event. They are not a form of psychic attack the average person, or even the average spiritual practitioner, is ever likely to hear about, or deal with. I have mentioned how difficult it is to control someone magically; to kill a person with magic is far more difficult, and is usually quite impossible.

A similar and only slightly less rare phenomenon is that of crazing by magic. This is when a magician launches a psychic attack intended to drive the victim insane. The person who commits this moral malpractice must be one who has well-developed magical abilities and no moral sense. People of this kind are very rare in any society, and they definitely do not go out looking for victims. Those who are able and willing to commit these kinds of crimes do so only for their own benefit. To have the kind of magical power and ability required, the magician must know the terrible karmic penalty they must pay. It is possible to hear of cases of magical murder and crazing, but whether or not the cause was actually the action of a magician is another story altogether. And as in all fields, where

PSYCHIC ATTACK

it is easy to claim credit for work you do not do, some magicians will take the credit for any accidents befall those whom they consider their enemies.

Having considered the various kinds of psychic attack, and having gained some understanding of how the mind works the process of psychic attack, we will now investigate the most blocking and limiting form of psychic attack, that which you do to yourself. Unfortunately, it is also the most common form of psychic attack.

7

PSYCHICALLY ATTACKING YOURSELF

The most common, and the most vicious, psychic attack that afflicts any person is the self-induced psychic attack. People attack themselves by a continuous stream of negative criticism, condemnation, and complaint, directed at themselves. People direct negativity at themselves because of their own negative perceptions of themselves, and their ingrained negative beliefs about themselves. Many people never voice any negativity, but they express it subconsciously as a part of the continual mental chatter of their mind. Even though they would never mention or speak their self-condemnation aloud, this continuous stream of self directed negativity would always take its toll upon its originator. Their self directed stream of negativity will produce as devastating a result as if they were the victim of the evil black magician of their favorite Gothic horror story. These people who attack themselves with their own negativity fall victim to their negative beliefs.

You create your experience with your beliefs. Your experience is based upon beliefs about yourself, your relationships, and the world you live in. These form the

PSYCHIC ATTACK

framework of the experiences you have in life. The beliefs you have about yourself are what form the basis of what you expect to happen to you over the course of your life. The expectations you have are the limits that regulate what will in fact manifest in your life. It is even said by some people that when you die you will enter into your beliefs.

Thoughts present in our conscious mind continually reinforce our beliefs. The expectations we have will bring to us what will come to us in this life. The beliefs within us are the roots of our thoughts, and on these beliefs our thoughts form the ideas we think. The thoughts we have continually bring to us, based on our beliefs and expectations, everything we experience in life. Once a belief has been accepted within us and its dogma set, the bars of our subconscious mind go up to oppose all changes of any kind. Yet our beliefs, as we shall see, can be changed through our efforts, to become more harmonious with what we desire to be the reality of our life.

Beliefs are the cause of our emotions. When we have an emotional reaction to anything it is because we have touched on a belief and an expectation. This has triggered our emotional reaction. Our beliefs, expectations, and subconscious emotions about ourselves, and about our life in general, are what govern the life we live. If we attempt to control our life by controlling our emotions, we will find that we are opposing the most powerful force within us with only our conscious mind. The opposition or the suppressions of the emotions within us by the willpower directed by our conscious mind is always futile. We would be using the conscious mind to oppose a basic force that makes us what we are. In such a struggle, the emotions will always win, even at the expense of the proper functioning of the conscious mind.

If we cannot control emotional reaction by the use of willpower and our conscious mind, we must look for a better way to gain the cooperation of this strong internal emotional power we have, so that we may apply it to assist us in our daily life. This may be accomplished by understanding and recognizing our beliefs, so that we can explain them to ourselves, and, when necessary, change them so what we believe unconsciously is in harmony with the physical world in

PSYCHICALLY ATTACKING YOURSELF

which we live. In this way, we can live in complete harmony with the world, being what we really are.

Any concept of belief we accept as being true is a belief we hold. When we begin to examine our beliefs, we must begin by recognizing that none of our ideas are necessarily true in the sense of being absolute divine truths. Everything we believe are we accept as true, is a belief, and all of our beliefs must be kept in our mind as being subject to change, based upon our life experience and our personal growth.

We may start investigating our beliefs by looking into how we came to hold some of our beliefs in the first place. At some point in our life, we accepted each of our beliefs as a real permanent truth. We must investigate who taught as each belief, and who was the agent who gave us each belief we hold. In some cases when we finally examine the reason we accepted the belief, we will find that the person who taught us the belief did so for their own, purely personal, reasons. We will find some beliefs are social constraints, which we accept to allow us to interrelate better with the society in which we live. In neither case can these believes be accepted as absolute truths, which is often what our subconscious mind holds them to be.

We can understand a child should accept their parents cautioned against crossing the street without holding their mother's hand, but when the same belief is held by an adult, it could cause a great deal of emotional anguish when they are forced to cross many streets without their mother, in their normal travel every day. Many similar limiting beliefs we accepted as children may still be operating within our subconscious mind, although as adults we have outgrown them. We must examine these beliefs and decide whether they should be allowed to continue to have any influence in our life.

To come to the full realization of the importance of belief in our life, we will have to look into ourselves and identify our basic beliefs. Once we find one, we must examine it. Then we must decide if we still wish to retain this belief, which may form the basic guide of our life. We must trace the complexity of our beliefs; one at a time, as far back as we can, to their source if possible. At their source, or as far back as we can trace them,

PSYCHIC ATTACK

we must either accept the belief as valid, or rejected it as being invalid. We must do this with each of the great many beliefs we hold.

There are three areas in which it is particularly important we search our beliefs, although we can and should continue far beyond these three areas. First, will we must examine any belief we hold that we do not fit into the real world, as we wish to experience it. This includes all beliefs that indicate a lack of self-worth, of our personal inadequacy, and all those beliefs dealing with self abasement. These are all false beliefs; they must be firmly rejected once their source is understood.

The second area in which beliefs are a direct blockage to our personal growth, literally a constant psychic attack upon us, is in the area of negative beliefs. Any negative belief we hold is a hindrance and limitation we never need in our life. Such negative beliefs include phrases that appear in our conversation, such as "I'm not good with numbers," and similar expressions. We can often identify the greatest area of our negative beliefs by carefully listening to our conversation. Once these negative beliefs are eliminated from our conversation, we will eventually eliminate them from our life. When we have eliminated negative belief from our life, we will find we are no longer limited in that area of our life. Our very real abilities will then expand accordingly.

The third area in which we have blockages and restrictions in our life, often posing as our beliefs, are those areas of our beliefs that deal with our friends, associates, and lovers. The beliefs we hold about those who share our life even to a slight extent can limit our own growth by limiting the way in which we react to them. Unless we are able to react to our family and friends in a positive manner, no matter what their reaction is to us, we are allowing them to have more control over us than we should be willing to give them. We are actually allowing them to control our emotions, as they are able to make us react emotionally to their words and actions. In a word, they are able to push our buttons.

Once we examine some of our beliefs in these areas, we should begin to examine other beliefs we may have. These

PSYCHICALLY ATTACKING YOURSELF

areas of belief includes such things as the examination of our accomplishments in life, looking at ourselves objectively to see what we have accomplished in terms of how it has benefited us, materially as well as in our spiritual growth. We can then investigate the beliefs we hold that make us feel guilty about any actions we take or have taken. In almost all cases, our feelings of guilt are without any true foundation. We must always remember that our emotion of feeling guilty about everything and anything is an excuse to keep us from accepting and profiting from the lesson of the experience. No one on this earth is perfect, and our Creator expects us to make mistakes and learn from these mistakes. If there were no learning there would be no reason for us to incarnate. Guilt is a poor substitute for learning and accepting the lessons of our experiences.

The best procedure for discovering the beliefs that we have is simplicity itself. You should ask yourself the question, "What do I believe about this?" Then, once you have answered that question, ask yourself, "Why do I believe that?" Next, ask questions, "Who taught me to believe that?" As well as asking, "Why did they teach me to believe it"?

Once you have answered these questions, you can change your belief by stating to yourself, "I used to believe that, but now I realize that it was an incorrect belief, so now I believe this."

Make a note of the new belief and carry the note with you for at least a week, to be certain you are acting on it. Keep this one new belief in the forefront of your mind during the week, enforcing it with your willpower at each opportunity. In this way, an incorrect belief is replaced with a correct belief. If you are able to change one incorrect belief every week for the next year, you will have improved your life in a major way by the end of the year.

One of the major false beliefs people have is that they must show internal worry and concern about every conceivable subject. A friend of mine admitted to me many years ago one of his chief worries had become that he had nothing to worry about. The average human mind is so conditioned to being full

PSYCHIC ATTACK

of chatter that if it should pause in its internal chatter, it will usually decide there is something wrong. In fact, the quiet mind is a developed mind, and it is never necessary for the mind to act, unless activity is required. We might compare the human mind to the engine of an automobile, although the human mental apparatus is far less important in the human system then the engine is to an automobile. People with almost no ability to think have rather normal lives, but no automobile can run without an engine. If the engine is operated constantly, it does not improve the functioning of the automobile. While human mind will not wear out from overuse, as an automobile engine will, it is not ever improved by being full of clutter or chatter.

Unfortunately, most people use the majority of their time to fill their mind with clutter and thoughts that have neither importance nor value in their lives. What difference does it make what you should have said to so-and-so? Why should the opinion of another person be so important to you that you are willing to distort your own life out of its proper course to secure their brief good impression? You must learn to see the events of your life in terms of their true value to you. The greatest task in your life, or in anyone else's life, is to grow closer to your creator. Every casual and unasked thought your conscious mind makes causes the fulfillment of that prime task to become more difficult, if not ultimately impossible. Until you are able to, "Stop Worrying And Start Living," you really will not have a true life of your own. You'll only be rehashing the experiences of others as you have viewed them through the clouded veils of your emotional perceptions. Despite the fact most people conduct their lives in this way, is not a good way to live. It is certainly not the best way to live on this earth.

Most people have within themselves a circle of negativity with which they constantly reinforce every negative thought or action that comes to them, or passes through their mind. As this circle operates, every negative thought reinforces every negative action, and every negative action reinforces every negative thought. Just as we understand how a productive positive belief pattern can be installed on the mind, as mentioned in the chapter about defense against common

PSYCHICALLY ATTACKING YOURSELF

psychic attack, so does the circle of negativity install negative belief patterns within our minds. If we are to free ourselves from negativity of thought in which we have immersed ourselves over the years, we must first break this circle of negativity within ourselves. Like breaking any other habit, it will require effort, and it will take time.

It is not enough to state that we shall henceforth be positive in thought word and deed. The circle of negativity which most of us have within ourselves has been built up over the years of our life. It will take us time and effort to break it down. It always requires work and effort on our part to break out of our self-inflicted internal negativity. Once we have succeeded in eliminating our negativity and self-depreciating internal conversations, we are well on our way to permanently breaking the circle of negativity. Once we never say or think, "I can't," or "I'm no good at," we have begun to turn our life away from negativity.

Once we have broken our negative speech habits, we can begin to break our negative thought patterns. This requires listening to other people speak, and in turn responding to what they have said with thoughtful speech of our own. Most people are so busy planning their replies to another's words in their mind; they do not listen to what is being said by the speaker. If we actually listen to what is being said, we are able to speak with more deliberation. Speaking with deliberation makes it possible for us to review our words and be certain that what we want to say is not only not negative, but it is what we actually want to say. Those who speak deliberately place more thought, and energy, into what they say. Those who hear deliberately spoken words place more faith in them.

Those who are flip conversationalist are usually thought to be funny and entertaining people, but few people take them seriously. Those who speak thoughtfully with a measured response to another person are usually taken far more seriously, even though the flip person may be more knowledgeable about the subject. I have seen this time and time again in my daily life, and so have most other people. When the usually flip person replies thoughtfully, his words

PSYCHIC ATTACK

immediately get a better reception by the person hearing them. This simple technique is often bandied about under the phrase, "Count to 10 before you reply." This phrase really works. Like so many of the techniques for self development found in our culture, this phrase, lies almost ignored by those who should heed it.

When negative thoughts enter the mind, as they always will, they should be gently pushed out. Using emotional force against negative thoughts will not rid you of them. Emotional force will only charge these negative thoughts with more emotional energy than they deserve. Simply refusing to think about negative thoughts, no matter how attractive they are, will work far more efficiently. You must ultimately take control of your mind, and this is the easiest and least painful way to begin to accomplish that goal.

You should push out negative or other undesired thoughts by refusing to entertain them. Turn your mind consciously to something else, preferably an entirely different subject. This technique requires a great deal of practice, but the results, in terms of increased mental clarity, are well worth it.

Refusing to dwell on negative thoughts requires that you be unconcerned from whence these thoughts originate. It does not really matter where these negative thoughts have their origin. They come either from your own mind, or are transmitted to you by someone else. The fact that you do not wish to entertain the thought is sufficient in itself. If another person has transmitted the thought to you, and if you are able to dismiss it without an emotional slur, you will find it must return to its sender, delivering its content of negativity upon their head.

We saw in the case of the couple we have called Ethel and George, that Ethel was badly beaten down by her own negative thoughts, which could not find a lodging place within George. She was being attacked by his directed negativity, just as she was being attacked by her own negativity. Thoughts must go somewhere, and if the person who is targeted for them will not accept it, the thought must return to the sender and lodge within them. Once you gently push thoughts from your mind,

PSYCHICALLY ATTACKING YOURSELF

refusing to entertain or display any curiosity about that thought, it must return to the one who sent it to you.

In the case of strongly directed thoughts of malefic intent, the results can be amusing for onlookers. I was boarding a bus with the daughter of a friend a few months ago when a woman bundled with packages appeared at the bus stop and directed a harsh thought of anger to us because we had boarded the bus. The daughter of my friend and I would not accept the woman's thought, which resulted in the anger being returned to her. She shouted at the bus driver who had also received some of her anger. He closed the door in her face and drove off leaving her raging in the street. This is only one example of how negative thoughts can make your life more difficult.

It is been said that the difference between one who approaches life in a positive manner and one who approaches life in a negative manner, is that the negative person looks at the hole in the doughnut while a positive person loads at the doughnut itself. We all make the choice every day as to what we wish to have in life, the doughnut or the doughnut hole. Unfortunately, many people seem to choose the hole over the doughnut.

With a negative approach to life, these people look for someone to blame for what they have called to themselves. They enter into the path of criticism, condemnation, and complaint. This sets them on a downhill road to ultimate disaster and despondency. It is only after death of these negative people they realize their mistake. At that point, when it is too late, they realize the opportunity they had missed in life due to their self-inflicted negativity.

Some people criticize others because they think they can motivate the person to make changes in their life. For the most part criticism only makes the person who is criticized resent the one who is criticizing them. Few people ever make a change in their life after being criticized by others. Offering a positive solution to the person, and teaching them how to accomplish the change they desire to make, is what makes changes in life.

Effective changes are made only when the person wants to make the changes themselves. Changes must be desired from

PSYCHIC ATTACK

within, they cannot be imposed from without.

As an example of this effect, there have been a number of suggestions for changing and improving a person's life made in this chapter. From experience, I know that only one out of 100 people who purchase this book will attempt to implement any of these changes. Yet I know that, again, from my own experience of doing precisely what I recommend in these pages in my years as a student, my life improved far beyond my expectations and beliefs of where it would or could go. It took me two years to make these changes in my own life, following no more instruction than is given in this chapter.

I freely give you the same information. Actually, I give a bit more information to you, hoping you are able to profit by the information as I was.

My sincere best wishes to you in your own efforts in self-improvement.

BEGINNING TO TRAIN YOUR MIND

Having a trained mind, a mind that is truly harmonized to the will of the creator of the universe, is undoubtedly the best possible protection against any form of psychic attack. A trained mind makes one invulnerable to any influence that is not more harmonized to the will of God than that of the possessor of the trained mind. Obtaining a trained mind is a task of the greatest difficulty. It requires long hours of work, and a great deal of effort to train the mind.

Many would-be magicians or occultist prefer to assume they have a trained mind, and that they can thereby enjoy its benefits. This is a much more pleasing belief for them, than spending time actually training their mind.

You may feel you have a trained mind when in fact you have managed only to discipline your mind. The child who never whines or cries from fear of its parent's wrath is not necessarily a trained child. The child is conditioned by fear it has not attained self-control. It has been disciplined, not trained. In the same way, should you be able to meditate for hours on end, it does not mean that you are able to focus your mind on

PSYCHIC ATTACK

anything other than your meditation. You may have been able to keep your mind free of extraneous thoughts while meditating, but like the fearful child, who when his parents are away is sure to get into some mischief, your mind may resume its chatter when your meditation period is finished.

I mentioned earlier that real spiritual power comes from real spiritual evolution. Training the mind alone is not developing the moral character that comes with true spiritual development. True spiritual power is the source of all true psychic power. As a person spiritualizes they gradually are able to place all their earthly emotions, desires, and ties, under the control of their true self. The person raises their earthly goals to the needs of their true, divine, nature. As this happens, the person ceases to entertain thoughts of envy, anger, hatred, greed, and jealousy, which are the common thoughts of those who have not begun to raise their spiritual nature.

When an individual is completely spiritualized, they do nothing for their human personality and everything for their divine personality. Such a person, shows nothing to friend or foe but an all-embracing love. A person in this position will never have any desire to perpetuate a psychic attack of any kind on anyone. They not only have no reason to attack anyone, but because they are operating from the viewpoint of their divine nature and its function incarnate on this earth, they will not interfere in the life of another human being. It is been said that the highest sages neither curse nor cure.

Below this optimum condition are found those who serve humanity, those who do good for others, when they are asked. Here are found the healers, teachers, and those who give aid and relief to fellow beings in distress, whether they act in this capacity as professional workers, teachers, doctors, surgeons, psychologists, or simply as neighbors of the distressed. Their position in life does not matter. They do what they can to reach relieve the sufferings of others. Because they recognize the true nature of distress, they often perform incomprehensible actions. They are rarely thought by their friends and neighbors to be very spiritual people. Because they know what the results of their actions will be, they assist in relieving the real distresses of humanity, usually one person at a time.

BEGINNING TO TRAIN YOUR MIND

Both of these classes of people must have trained minds to perform their functions in the world. This requires they have to have trained their minds. They have received spiritual training in their present incarnation. Of no other class of people is real spiritual training required. To reach either of these places in the divine scheme of things, true spiritual training is required in the present life, through the offices of a living spiritual teacher.

Next come those people who are generally recognized by the world is being psychic or as having unusual abilities and strange or mysterious powers. These are people who may have trained their minds in past incarnations, and who may be more or less spiritually developed. These people usually have subconscious abilities, but they have not received true spiritual training in this life, and they do not have any true or deep knowledge of the divine realities. Their psychic perceptions are so strong they are usually certain they are among God's chosen people. Their high opinion of themselves often reveals the true condition of their supposed spirituality.

These psychic wonders may spend their lives doing what is apparently good. This results in their sometimes doing real good and sometimes not doing real good. Because they are not harmonized to the divine realities, they are perfectly capable of doing great evil with the intention of doing good. The training that they have received in past lives has only been of such a nature as to discipline their minds and place them on the path of spiritual growth. In their present existence, they seek and obtain the use of various powers, and in some cases the control of various forces of the universe. Because these people do not have deep understanding of the divine reality, they are not able to readily distinguish what they do. Many times a part of their divine nature is manifesting, but usually their human will is not surrendered to their creator.

While these people have incarnated to complete the process of their spiritual training and advancing themselves on the path, their desires of the Earth will frequently lure them completely away from the spiritual path. They may actually lose more spiritual power, because of their incarnation, than they can gain. It is from the ranks of these people that those known as

PSYCHIC ATTACK

great magicians, learned occultists, and psychics, those who are wonder workers, are drawn. Many lifetimes can be spent in this state of blessed but powerful ignorance. It is only when the lack of true spirituality manifests within them, and the debts incurred in this state have been paid, that the person who finds themselves in this state is able to turn their hearts and minds toward their creator and resume the process of spiritual growth and elevation.

The person with a trained mind has few or no belief patterns within their mind. They hold nothing sacred except their creator. They do not even share the generally agreed beliefs of humanity as a whole. They understand the processes of belief as a tool that can be used for a specific purpose, not as something that is a necessity in the daily affairs of their life. This is a completely different concept of belief from any that is usually taught. It is not subject to logical or rational explanation, no matter how much this additional verbiage might be desired.

Individuals with a trained mind have no negative programming of any kind within their subconscious. All of the mental belief programming they have is programming which they have placed within their minds for a specific purpose. Their mental programming may be erased and reprogrammed or modified whenever the occasion may call for changes. When a belief program has served its purpose, it can be erased completely. One of the conclusions that may be drawn from this is that just as there are no beneficial beliefs, there are no beneficial habit programs. Any mental program is based upon beliefs. The operation of an action or a reaction through programmed response means the one acting or reacting is really just drawing on their beliefs to decide just which of the many programs is to be played, to accomplish or to respond to any particular situation.

Implicit in these abilities is the ability to control all of the thoughts that enter the trained mind. This indicates the mental energy of the thinking processes are completely under the control of the person doing the thinking. The development of this ability begins with learning to stop the mentation process, resulting in the cessation of the continuous metal conversation

BEGINNING TO TRAIN YOUR MIND

that occurs in the chatter of a mind operating in the free association of reverie. Most human beings pass through life with their minds filled with whatever random thoughts present themselves to their mind. The process of reverie is dependent on the amount of excess emotional energy trapped in the memory of the subconscious mind. Until a person can learn to stop this chatter completely, it is useless for them to believe they have control over their mind.

The trained mind has thoughts presented to the conscious mind by the subconscious mind for acceptance or rejection, through the harmonization of the two facets of the mind. When influence from the nonphysical universe presents itself to the subconscious part of the trained mind, the conscious mind is immediately notified. It is literally asked if it wishes to accept the thought. Should the rational conscious mind decide to reject the thought, no part of it will remain within the subconscious mind. Such a mind is not susceptible to influence from outside itself.

Two excellent books may be used to begin the process of training the mind. They will take the student to the point of at least recognizing that the road has a beginning, and they will assist them on their way, but no one has ever received enlightenment from books. These books are both by Mouniu Sadhu, they are Concentration and Meditation. Reading the first part of Concentration, up to the beginning of the exercises, will at least indicate what is expected of them in the process of mental training. Once all of the exercises in Concentration have been completed, the student should work their way through Meditation. This process will take at least two full years of dedicated effort, and usually more. The books have their own instructions, I shall only say that if one is not able to follow the instructions within the books, they were not intended to make much progress in training their mind.

From the order in which this is written, it would seem that I am advocating the removal of all of the emotional memory, beliefs, and all negative programming before the training of the mind has begun. This is the procedure I feel works best in practice. Once you enter into the mental discipline phase of

PSYCHIC ATTACK

mental training, there will be a new flood of beliefs and programming to deal with. No matter how much is removed prior to mental training, the surface is all that can actually be skimmed.

The work outlined above usually requires a teacher of some merit to accomplish. The teacher is always a live human being who speaks your language and who can communicate to you in a small group setting, as well as face-to-face in a personal setting. There is an old saying that when the student is ready the teacher will appear. This saying is still true. It should be modified to mention that the student will always receive the kind of teacher they deserve. As has recently been pointed out by a leading spiritual teacher, the teacher also receives those students he deserves.

Those who have earned the right to listen to discarnate spirits speak through a medium will find that kind of teacher. Those who have earned access to sit at the feet of a guru who sits on a platform and receives the worship of an adoring multitude will find the proper guru for them. Those who have earned the right to more personal instruction will find that some of these living teachers are good, some bad, some indifferent, while a few are excellent.

Those who are disciples of the teacher or guru who does not speak their language should notice that those who the teacher or guru teaches privately are usually those who speak the same language as the guru, and who are from his same ethnocultural background. The full understanding of the implications of this would make the absorption into the American mainstream of India's leading exports, gurus, considerably more difficult. Americans like to participate in and enjoy mass movements. Unfortunately, there is no such thing as a mass movement toward spiritual growth.

Further abilities of the trained mind include the identification of the will as a separate constituent of the individuality. This places the will in the position of being the directing force which may use the rational thoughts of the thinking machine as the basis for its action, or which may choose to use, with equal ability, another part of the human nonphysical constitution.

BEGINNING TO TRAIN YOUR MIND

What is called free will in Christian doctrine should be referred to as *relatively free will*, because of the common tendency to regard the willpower as able only to enforce the decisions of the rational mind. That the willpower can also respond to the demands of the erotic animal instinctual nature can be noted by observing the actions and behavior of those who we usually say have no willpower. They have willpower, it may be weak or undeveloped, but it is certainly present.

The willpower of the individual human being is also able to select from a variety of sources the solution to any particular problem that faces the person at any time. It can then solve that problem in accordance with the solutions the rational mind desires to utilize, through focusing the energy of the emotional nature toward the solution of the difficulty. If the emotional energies are bound up within the person they will be constrained, not free to be applied to the solution of a problem that may present itself to the person at the time. In most instances, it is blocking of the emotional energy that inhibits the person from the successful completion of their destiny they have chosen in their life. The average person spends more time dwelling in the past and anticipating the future than they do living their life in the present.

Another characteristic of the trained mind is the ability to non-judgmentally interrelate with others. This is always blocked in the untrained person by matters of self-concern and the egoic and animal instinctual drives. You must understand and practice concern for others as a moral duty before you can abandon self-concern. You must understand your animal instinctual drive, and its desires, without either denying them through suppressing them or denying in a false desire to spiritualize by supposedly setting yourself above them. You must understand them and realize their origin within yourself. Only then can you can control them in a harmonious manner, without riding roughshod over your animal body to the point where it ceases to serve you as it should.

In the process of interrelating with others, you do not necessarily have auric vision, communication with the spirits of the dead or other occult effects. These strange and wonderful

PSYCHIC ATTACK

experiences, from the realms of the psychic research societies and the occult, and little to do with being able to look at another human being and nonjudgmentally assess their place in the universe. This is correctly seeing the individual. Psychic and occult effects are often the perception of the viewer's sense of self-importance transmitted by the sense of self-importance of the person seen, through the veil of the viewer's self-deception.

The person with a trained mind has a desire to work only in accordance with their destiny in that particular incarnation. They have no other goal or desire in life. Until they have lost their sense of self-importance, they may drift a bit, but they will usually return to the correct track in life after they lose belief in their self-importance. A sense of self-importance is an expression of the real ego. It is that which makes one think that they are unique from any other part of the divine creation. Until you realize you are an integral part of the entire creation in your guts, rather than in your mind, you will still have your ego interests and your animal instinctual nature blocking you from accomplishing your true destiny.

As an aside it might be worthwhile pointing out that those who are blocking themselves from there true destiny usually turn to either drugs or alcohol to loosen the bonds which hold the spirit imprisoned in the flesh. Once they return to their path in life, they can easily lose his addiction to alcohol, as Alcoholics Anonymous has been practicing for a number of years. People go off their path in life by the actions of the Earth, or the flesh, on their spirit. People regain their path in life through the action of their spirit on the flesh.

I mention this particular facet of human behavior because those who present themselves as spiritual teachers, gurus, occult masters, and so forth who are addicted to the use of either alcohol or drugs are not what they claim. The enthusiasm of their followers is not important; these people are simply people off their true path in life. They may or may not return to their true path in life, but so long as they are dependent upon drugs or alcohol, they have no right to pretend to teach, or even to advocate spiritual growth.

BEGINNING TO TRAIN YOUR MIND

The individual with a trained mind is always typified by the clarity of their thoughts, their emotions, and their actions. They present a uniform personality to the world, one that is not swayed by the daily trifles of life. When they do something, they do it. They are not ever people who leave incomplete actions lying about to force them to return to complete unfinished tasks later.

9

EXERCISES USEFUL FOR THOSE WHO WISH TO TRAIN THEIR MINDS

The results of these exercises enter into everything that comes after them, so you should carefully master them. You will find the abilities you gain from these exercises will be very useful to you in your daily life, as well as developing your magical abilities. You should practice these exercises every day, twice a day, if it is at all possible for you to do so.

The exercises should be followed until mastered, in the order given:

I

The purpose of this exercise is to assist you in learning to be silent so that you are able to listen effectively

For one hour every day, when you are in the presence of other people, you are to refrain from initiating any conversation. You may reply to others, and you may continue any conversation started by others, but you may not begin a conversation, make any comments to any ongoing conversation, or comment on any remark made by anyone else.

EXERCISES TO DEVELOP THE MIND

II

The purpose of this exercise is to assist you in removing physical tension from your life

You are to master the art of relaxing your physical body. This begins by lying down with the palms of your hands up, and consciously willing your physical body to relax, while ignoring the chatter in your mind. You may begin by relaxing one extremity at a time telling yourself for example to relax your toes, relax your feet and so on, up to your head.

There are any numbers of systems for relaxing yourself, and it does not matter which system you use, but the object of this is to relax your body, while ignoring your mind. Once you can completely relax, your body at will you are making progress. The object of this exercise is to be able to completely relax your body at will. This exercise has nothing at all to do with silencing your mind.

You should be able to relax your body for two periods of fifteen minutes a day. This is your goal.

III

The purpose of this exercise is to maximize your breathing

Every one thinks they know how to breath, but few people actually do. Many people breath desiring to obtain the greatest possible chest expansion. This is exactly the wrong way to breath. When a baby is born they breathe with their diaphragm, and it is diaphragm breathing which you must return to, should you wish to maximize your human economy.

Think of your body as a steam engine. The food you eat is the fuel furnishing you with energy, but in order to burn the fuel, you must also have oxygen, which you get from the air you breath. Unless you breathe with your diaphragm, you will not be bringing in enough air to efficiently burn the fuel, the food, you are easting.

PSYCHIC ATTACK

Place your hand on your belly and pant like a dog. The motion is that of your diaphragm. Now breathe, inhaling as your diaphragm draws in the air, and exhale as your diaphragm pushed the air out.

Mastering breathing with your diaphragm takes time and practice. All singers must master this exercise, and it will produce favorable changes in your voice and speech as well. You should mentally agree with yourself you will breathe with your diaphragm at all times. Whenever you feel you are not breathing in this way, you should correct yourself. In time, this will make breathing with your diaphragm the normal way you breathe.

IV

The purpose of the following exercises is to develop your focus and concentration.

The following exercises are used to develop your ability to focus and concentrate your mind. Chose one of the two exercises and stick with it for at least six months, performing it twice a day for at least five or ten minutes each time. Once you have mastered one of these exercises, go ahead and master the other one.

NOTE: When performing either of these exercises, ignore any random thoughts that may pass through your mind. Just pay no attention at all to them. Do not be concerned about blanking your mind, or stopping your thoughts. That is not the purpose of either of these exercises. Just focus completely on the exercise and ignore anything that may pass through your mind.

BREATHING CONCENTRATION EXERCISE

Sit comfortably, as you inhale, and exhale consciously. As you inhale, mentally say to yourself, 'In comes the air.' As you exhale, mentally say to yourself, 'Out goes the air.' Focus all of your attention on your breathing as you practice this exercise.

EXERCISES TO DEVELOP THE MIND

CANDLE CONCENTRATION EXERCISE

Light a small birthday candle and concentrate all of your attention on the flame. Observe the flame as closely as you can, until the candle burns out. Do not allow anything to distract your attention from the candle flame.

V

The purpose of this exercise is to master the ability to pay attention, thus fulfilling an internal need, as well as learning about other people.

For human beings, attention is a necessity. We seek it, we need it, and we must give it to receive it. Once we understand the necessity of giving and receiving attention, we can make our path in life an easier one. We must view attention as a commodity, something we must exchange with others. Once we understand the necessity of attention, and look at it as something we must exchange with others to benefit from, we can realize that our understanding and control of attention is something we must master to succeed in life.

With a controlled and focused mind, we will be more adept at paying attention to others, and as a result, we can more easily satisfy our own attention needs.

The next time you are speaking to someone, look intently at the bridge of their nose and concentrate on them as you speak to them. This is intensely paying attention to them. In most cases, they will return the attention you pay to them by paying attention to you. In some cases, they will avoid paying attention to you, by shifting their eyes, or by looking away. If this is what they do, your opinion of them, and your interchange with them will be a great deal different than it would have been if they were paying attention to you in return. This little exercise will give you some insights into the art of paying attention to others, and gaining attention from them in return.

PSYCHIC ATTACK

Observation
Learning how to see

I have often spoken about developing the art of observation as mentioned in one of Kipling's books as "Kim's Game." This observation game teaches how to see and observe physical things. Another similar game is the "Shopping Game," where a store window is observed for a short time and the individual tries to recall all of the items in the window. If you really wish to develop your powers of observation, and increase your ability to pay attention to others, you should concentrate on playing these games for a few months. You will probably be amazed at how much more you see of what is happening around you.

Another useful exercise is to note the eye color of everyone you meet. When you write their address in your book, note their eye color as being Bl - blue or Br – Brown. There are no other possible eye colors in human beings. The varieties are all based on Blue or Brown.

Carefully noting the persons eye color will have the additional advantage of making the person think you like them and are sincerely interested in developing a friendship with them. However, this is not a sexual allure, it is more of a business or social allure.

Additional Information

Remedies for Common Psychic Attack

There are two ways of preventing or dealing with psychic attack. The first is by wearing or carrying a protective charm, and the second is by mastering the art of resisting these influences. Of the two, the latter is far more difficult to master. So it is probably best to carry a charm at all times.

Saints cards are one form of charm, as are symbolic horns, herbs, or a variety of other things. A protective charm linked to the individual's cultural base is best to use, as it will have the greatest effect. An example of a cultural charm is wearing a nail, usually a cut nail, in the hair. Some charms are prepared for this purpose, such as the Cuban asavache, which is to prevent Malochia and prevent or lighten any curse directed at the one who wears it.

Mastering the art of resisting negative influences comes through training the mind, although mental training solves this difficulty only when the training is almost completed. Refusing to accept a curse might be said to be turning the other cheek, as when a curse is refused, it returns to its sender

Curing a Common Psychic Attack

For the most part, common psychic attacks should be treated as if the attack were malochia or the evil eye. This is the most common form of psychic attack, and it is the one most noticeable to the recipient. Other psychic attacks can go on for years, undermining the person until there is a "sudden crash," often into poverty, destitution, and personal ruin. Malochia has a more direct or instant effect, revealing itself as a sudden pain, a headache, or an immediate physical debility. Malochia cannot postpone its action or delay announcing its presence.

There are several cures for Malochia; some may be self-administered, while another person must administer others. Among the self-administered cures are the salt rub, the egg

PSYCHIC ATTACK

rub, and several baths. All of these should be performed on the nude body of the victim by the victim themselves.

A Salt Rub For Malochia

Take about a tablespoon of salt and rub it over the sternum the area between the breasts, rubbing the salt from about the navel to the base of the throat, and going up and down several times. This is best accomplished in the shower or bathtub, as excess salt will fall down the front of the body while this rub is being done.

Salt may also be rubbed on the temples, as well as on any other part of the body that seems to be debilitated. I have heard of one person who rubs salt into their hair before they shower or bathe. They believe this removes any negativity or spiritual influences that may be present. I have not tried this myself, but it seems to me it would work.

An Egg Rub For Malochia

Rub an egg over the affected part of the body, while praying that any negativity be removed from the person. The head should receive special attention, and a final cross made over the head, from ear top to ear top, then from the back of the head to the forehead. In a few severe cases, several eggs may be used. If an egg breaks in the course of this rub put it in the toilet and use another egg to finish the rub.

Rubbing an egg on the sternum is also a good idea, as it is the sternum which often receives the negativity of a psychic attack, whether it is a general negativity being sent out by a disgruntled person, or a directed attack sent by someone angry with the individual. In fact using an egg on the head and the sternum is probably the best practice for daily or weekly general cleansing from negativity.

I have heard several people have successfully used an egg rub on ill or out of sort's animals, particularly their pet dogs. As animals will often take on the negativity directed at their masters, particularly when there is a bond of affection between them, I do not find this surprising. I recommend it as a first aid measure for animals showing signs of odd behavior.

Baths To Remove Malochia

The Beer Bath -

Foremost among all the baths used to remove negative spiritual influences is the beer bath. In this bath a tub of luke warm or cool water is drawn, and between three 12 Oz bottles of beer - or a quart of beer - is added to the water. A tablespoon of salt is also added, and the bath stirred.

The person bathing then enters the bath and immediately ducks into the bath so it covers them completely. They then remain in the bath for between three to seven minutes, - the longer the better – pouring water over themselves and immersing themselves fully between three to five times.

On coming out of the tub, they allow themselves to air dry, although they may wrap a towel around their hair. The residue of the bath should stay on them at least overnight, although allowing the residue to remain a whole day has also been recommended.

You may notice these instructions are a bit different from those in my book Spiritual Cleansing. I have added some options; because of complaints, I received from other practitioners, saying they were not taught to take this bath as I had prescribed. This bath may be taken in any number of ways, so long as the basics are observed. These are, several complete immersions, with air drying, and allowing the residue to remain on the body for a time. To my mind, the longer in the tub pouring water over yourself, and having five immersion, as well as allowing the residue to stab on over night will produce the best results. However, this seems to be subject to argument.

An Orange Bath for Women -

The peelings of a number of oranges boiled slowly for a few minutes, and the water then allowed to cool, will produce an extraction of orange oil from the orange peel. Adding this to a tub of water, sitting in the tub for five to seven minutes, immersing yourself five times, will assist any woman in

PSYCHIC ATTACK

removing the negativity from her that others may have sent her. This bath will also allow her radiate a more feminine vibration something those women who have been exposed to negativity will certainly appreciate.

I also have learned that frequently taking this bath will cause women to be more attractive to the men they meet. Apparently, it makes them look and seem to be more feminine.

Salt Bath -

A salt bath, like a salt rub, frees the person from minor negativity. This may also be accomplished by pouring a couple of cups of salt water over your head in the shower. A tablespoon of salt is all it takes, so you can add this to your regular bath water.

Please do not expect this minor remedy to have great effects. It will not remove a curse, or great negativity.

There are several other baths in my book Spiritual Cleansing, as well as in Century of Spells and A Spiritual Workers Spell Book. Please do not believe that taking any of these baths will change your life for the better in a permanent way. These baths are to help you, not do your work for you.

37,512   Gr. 10.6
(122/4=30.5)

PSYCHIC ATTACK

Printed in Great Britain
by Amazon